# THE OFFICIAL

## *Agatha Christie*®

# PUZZLE BOOK

# THE OFFICIAL

## *Agatha Christie*®

## PUZZLE BOOK

Agatha Christie Limited

LAURENCE KING

First published in Great Britain in 2024 by
Laurence King, an imprint of The Orion
Publishing Group Ltd, Carmelite House,
50 Victoria Embankment, London EC4Y 0DZ

An Hachette UK Company

10 9 8 7 6 5 4 3 2 1

A CIP catalogue record for this book is
available from the British Library.

ISBN (Trade Paperback) 978 1 3996 2793 1

Printed and bound in the United States

www.laurenceking.com
www.orionbooks.co.uk

# CONTENTS

*A Puzzling Mystery Awaits . . .*

*All Shall Be Revealed . . .*

SOLVE ME

# CHAPTER 1

# The Mysterious Affair at Styles

# THE GREAT DETECTIVE

*The Mysterious Affair at Styles* was the first English case of its kind investigated by Monsieur Hercule Poirot, whose success as a detective in his native Belgium was legendary.

Words linked to detection are hidden in this grid and can run up, down, across, backwards or diagonally. Beware: your detective skills are still needed when you've found all the words. Take the unused letters reading down in the first four columns to make a famous quality attributed to the great detective.

```
S F F C S S U O I C I P S U S
S D I S G U I S E B T R A I L
E L N N L A O L I T R T O A G
N C D E G E I L S O V C N L U
T I I L P E A E T S E I T I I
I C G L D G R C R T M V R A L
W N O L O R E P A I I N U S T
Y T Q N A P N G R C R O E E Y
T Y R U S D I C C I C C R R V
I T F N E T E H O X N C E H I
T T I I S S A Y U E E T N C C
N L E E R R T B D S S H S R T
E E V S G E Z I L Y E A R A I
D N Y E A G V A M E U L C E M
I N N O C E N T C E P S U S D
```

| | |
|---|---|
| ALIAS | INQUEST |
| ALIBI | INSPECTOR |
| ARREST | INVESTIGATE |
| CASE | LIED |
| CHARGE | MYSTERY |
| CLUE | PLOT |
| CONSTABLE | POLICE |
| CONVICT | SEARCH |
| CRIME | SECRET |
| CRIMINAL | SUSPECT |
| DISGUISE | SUSPICIOUS |
| EVIDENCE | TRAIL |
| FIND | TRUE |
| FINGERPRINTS | VERIFY |
| GUILTY | VICTIM |
| IDENTITY | WITNESS |
| INNOCENT | |

# CONNECTING ROOMS

This plan shows the first floor of Styles as recorded by Captain Hastings. Some rooms have connecting doors, some rooms have a single door in and out. You are present at Styles to help Monsieur Poirot investigate.

Assume that you have already entered one of the rooms. You can never enter a room more than once.

◇ You open the door of this room and step into the corridor.

◇ You then turn right and open the next door that you come to.

◇ You go into the room and then open an interconnecting door and move on.

◇ Satisfied with your observations, you exit and cross the corridor to inspect a room with a single door.

◇ Moving left down the corridor, you enter the table gallery.

◇ You turn into a corridor where you examine in turn the three rooms which overlook the courtyard.

◇ Crossing the corridor, you open three more doors on your journey.

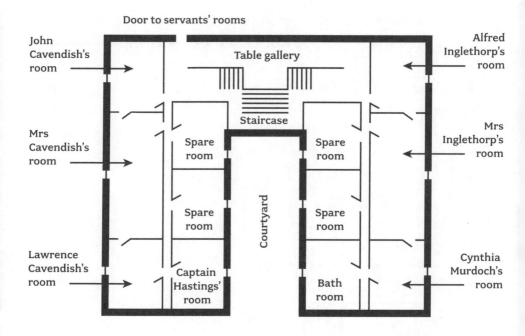

John Cavendish's room

Door to servants' rooms

Table gallery

Alfred Inglethorp's room

Mrs Cavendish's room

Staircase

Spare room

Spare room

Mrs Inglethorp's room

Spare room

Courtyard

Spare room

Lawrence Cavendish's room

Captain Hastings' room

Bath room

Cynthia Murdoch's room

You end up in a room. Which one?

You did not inspect the bathroom.
Which other room did you not call at?

In which room did you start your search?

# SECRET CODE

Dr Bauerstein was an expert in poisons and befriended Mary Cavendish at Styles. **Can you work out the coded message below?**

You can move from letter to letter in any direction, except diagonally.

| O | N | T | S | U | E | V |
|---|---|---|---|---|---|---|
| W | G | E | T | M | R | O |
| Y | A | W | A | D | E | C |
| A | S | S | O | D | I | S |
| S | A | N | O | N | H | A |
| P | E | L | B | E | I | V |
| O | S | S | I | E | B | E |

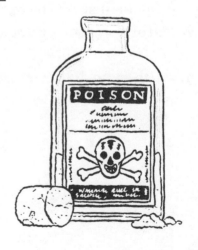

# PIECE TOGETHER

The household at Styles was instructed not to waste anything, including paper, as a contribution to the war effort. Therefore, confidential material had to be burned or torn into much smaller pieces. Here are fragments of a letter which has met this very same fate.

**Can you put the pieces back together and work out the message?**

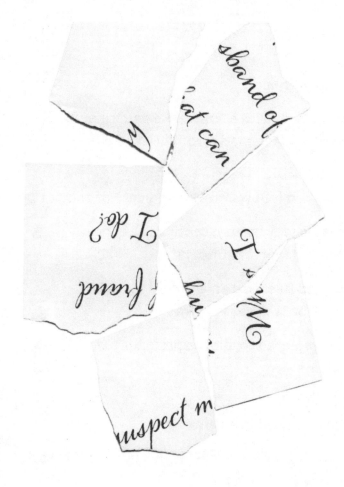

# MAKE A WILL

Two circles. One list of clues. It's up to you to work out which word goes in which grid.

Grid A has **MAKE** as the starter word. Grid B's first word is **WILL**. Solve the clues so that each answer is one letter different from the previous one. All answers have four letters. The last word has one letter different from the first in each grid. **Can you help make out a will?**

## CLUES

1.  A legal document
    * Create or build

2.  A garden tool with a comb-like end for smoothing soil
    * A barrier often made from brick

3.  Prolonged cry of grief
    * This word follows first, to indicate of class or quality

4.  Learn this way by constantly repeating
    * Delay a departure until later

5.  Food used to entice an animal
    * Decomposes, wastes away

6.  Money required to allow a prisoner's temporary release
    * Rodents

7.  Small rugs
    * A sphere used in a game

8.  This word goes after 'check' in a game of chess
    * Slender beak of a bird

## Grid A

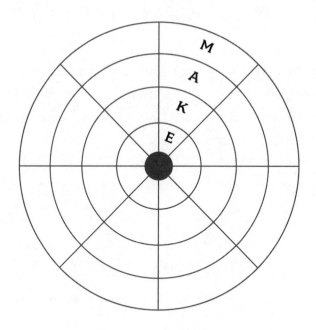

## Grid B

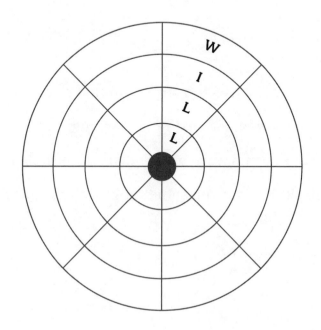

# ACTING ON INSTINCT

Solve the clues and write your answers across in the larger grid. As you work your way through, keep in mind the shaded letters in order to complete the smaller grid, which includes some advice from the great man himself.

'Instinct is a marvellous thing,' mused Poirot. 'It can neither be ...'

**CLUES**

1. Person appointed to carry out the terms of a will

2. Cynthia Murdoch worked in the dispensary here in Tadminster

3. An old friend of Poirot invited to Styles by John Cavendish

4. Harmed or killed by taking a toxic substance such as strychnine

5. Subject studied by Lawrence Cavendish when he wanted to be a doctor

6. A storyteller, such as the answer to clue 3

7. Very confusing or perplexing, as were many of Poirot's cases

8. Distinctive outfits worn by members of the military

9. A small piece torn from something, such as part of a will or a piece of clothing

10. Famous, celebrated

| | | | | | | | | |
|---|---|---|---|---|---|---|---|---|
| 1 | | | | | | | | |
| 2 | | | | | | | | |
| 3 | | | | | | | | |
| 4 | | | | | | | | |
| 5 | | | | | | | | |
| 6 | | | | | | | | |
| 7 | | | | | | | | |
| 8 | | | | | | | | |
| 9 | | | | | | | | |
| 10 | | | | | | | | |

| | | | | | | | | | | | |
|---|---|---|---|---|---|---|---|---|---|---|---|
| | | | | | | | | | | | |
| | | | | | | | | | | | |

# POISONED CRYPTIC

In this decidedly tricky cryptic crossword, five answers are the names of deadly poisons.

**Can you emulate the brilliant Monsieur Poirot and fill in the grid?**

## ACROSS

3 Correspond to firelighter (5)
7 Buy tea well stirred; it is a thing of loveliness (6)
8 Miss Howard is evenly balanced (6)
10 The inch sentry moved made poison (10)
11 Rail about teller of untruths (4)
12 Different tones in sparkling gem (5)
13 Cute prose translated to start legal proceedings (9)
16 This miss I only discovered on military expedition (7)
21 Brother's head covering is toxic! (9)
22 Stray when food carriers overturn (5)
23 Control legacy document (4)
24 Leaves remain on them as genres veer away (10)
26 Finder finds pal (6)
27 Hides the truth seen at the window (6)
28 Votes cast on cooker (5)

## DOWN

1 Add tea, we hear, to tea set having left a valid 23 across (7)
2 Aunt boy disturbed is very resilient (7)
3 Legend comes to light from my theory (4)
4 Hear, we hear in this place (4)
5 Hair below the edge of garment — poison! (7)
6 Lineage beginning with lady, nasty though she appears (7)
9 Crops mice add to point zero used to look at close quarters (11)
14 Put an end to broken pots (4)
15 As a favour I choose to reveal Mrs Inglethorp to be very wealthy (4)
17 Pay it or destroy garden decoration (7)
18 Kill with set exposes cooking utensil (7)
19 Acres in disarray unearth poison (7)
20 Nice day for finding poison! (7)
24 Send round the conclusions (4)
25 While listening I begin to understand mocking taunt (4)

# CANDLELIGHT

Candles were used as a source of light at Styles when the murder of Emily Inglethorp took place. Below you will find a stock of candles, all piled on top of one another. In which order must you pick them up so that you are always taking the top candle off the pile?

Note that the numbers are here to help you identify the candles (I thought you might need help on this one, it is marvellously boggling). The numbers DO NOT refer to the order in which the candles are picked up, that would be much too easy.

**How many — if any — of the candles has a number that DOES match the order that it was top of the pile?**

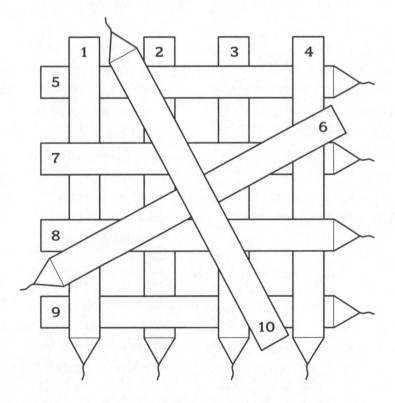

# COMME ÇA

Poirot is talking to himself, as he often does. It is not unusual for him to do so in both English and French, all mixed together. He is currently musing over several dates, which he deems to be significant. The sentences seem to make no sense at all, but there are numbers hidden there. It might help if you spoke the sentences out loud, like Poirot. Can you translate the details?

1. I need to know what happened to those petrol cans. If the boat sank I would never forgive myself.

2. The brake van could be found at the rear of the train as a safety feature. Accidents may not cease, but may be reduced.

3. The doctor says that all is now going well. He is all set to discharge the patient without further delay.

# ALL ABOUT STYLES

In this puzzle, words read across and down. Slot them into their correct places in the grid.

**But be mindful: there is only one correct way to do this.**

## 3 LETTERS

ASK
BOX
LAW
PAN
SPY
WAR

## 4 LETTERS

CUPS
FEUD
JAPP
MARY
WILL

## 5 LETTERS

BEARD
DEATH
ESSEX
WIDOW

## 6 LETTERS

ALFRED
ARTHUR
BOTTLE
FRIEND
LETHAL
POIROT
POWDER

## 7 LETTERS

CYNTHIA
EXPLAIN
HERCULE
LIBRARY
REFUGEE

## 8 LETTERS

HASTINGS
MEDICINE

## 9 LETTERS

CAVENDISH
DETECTION

## 10 LETTERS

BAUERSTEIN
INGLETHORP
SPIRIT LAMP
STEPMOTHER
STRYCHNINE

## 12 LETTERS

COUNTRY MANOR
SCOTLAND YARD
STYLES ST MARY

## 16 LETTERS

LEASTWAYS COTTAGE

Dear Aunt Mary,

Greenway is as we expected: a treasure trove of Agatha Christie's life, the library a celebration of her works. Our shared delight in mystery stories over the years has made me feel at home, and I must thank you for your encouragement to join as Greenway's new librarian.

I have to admit, though, that things here are not quite what I expected. I arrived at the library today at nine o'clock sharp, so that Mrs Ashmore, who has been librarian at Greenway for more than twenty-five years now, could begin showing me what I am to do. I waited patiently for her to arrive and by half past was starting to think there must have been some sort of misunderstanding.

I hope I might be excused for looking through Mrs Ashmore's desk, as it will be my own soon enough. Under stacks of papers and mountains of hardback books, my eyes caught hold of a copy of *The Mysterious Affair at Styles*. The book seemed to be a rather odd shape and I found it hiding a bundle tied neatly together with string.

After teasing a few pages apart, I could see a collection of what looked like different kinds of puzzles. I studied them as closely as I could without untying the package, keeping an eye on the door in case Mrs Ashmore appeared.

However, it feels as though the puzzles have been left purposefully for me. A welcome present from Mrs Ashmore, perhaps? In her mysterious absence, they are all I have to go on.

I will do my best to uncover the answers, in the hope that they give me some of my own. It is far from ideal that one has completely stumped me, however. Could I ask for your help? You always were brilliant at guessing whodunnit. I've tried to write it out as best I can below.

When I write next, I hope all will be explained and I'll be an old hand as librarian here.

Your nephew,

Charles

# IN DISGUISE

---

This is a traditional symmetrical crossword (without the clues, did you think it was going to be that easy?), but the black squares you also might expect have been replaced by other letters.

---

Can you see through the disguise, put back the black squares and produce the correct crossword?

| | | | | | | |
|---|---|---|---|---|---|---|
| T | W | O | M | U | S | E |
| A | H | A | G | A | E | A |
| P | O | P | U | L | A | R |
| A | D | I | E | L | L | E |
| D | R | E | S | S | E | D |
| B | A | I | T | E | A | I |
| A | G | E | D | A | R | T |

# CHAPTER 2

# The Murder at the Vicarage

TELEPHONE EXCHANGE

LOSING THE PLOT

QUOTE LINES

GOSSIP

HYMN NUMBERS

WORD LADDER

GRAVESTONES

BEAT THE CLOCK

DOUBLE CROSS

THE CURATE'S COLLECTION

# TELEPHONE EXCHANGE

The list of telephone numbers below has been written on the notepad next to the telephone. The numbers belong to people attending the village fête (where, undoubtedly, tea and cakes will be served). There has been a threat that someone at the village hall may be in danger.

Use the numbers and the telephone dial to work out how to avoid an untimely death . . .

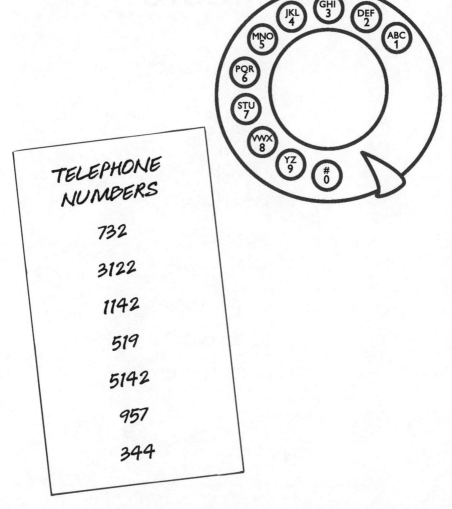

TELEPHONE
NUMBERS

732

3122

1142

519

5142

957

344

# LOSING THE PLOT

The church needs to sell off land so that new houses can be built. The vicarage wants to retain an area of garden and divide the existing large garden into three building plots. Each new plot and the retained garden area must be the same shape and size. Don't lose the plot and divide up the land.

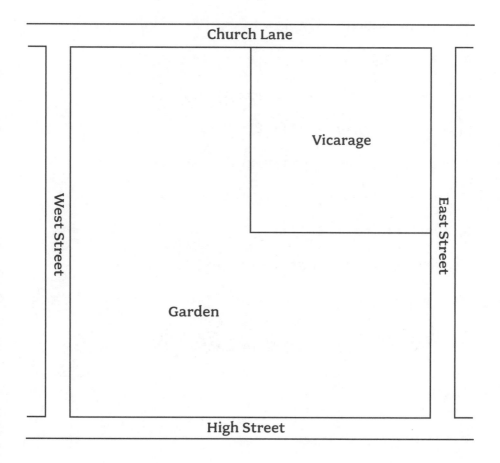

# QUOTE LINES

Solve the clues, slotting the numbers which follow them in the correct places in the grids opposite. Complete the quotation which begins, 'There is no detective in England equal to . . .'

**CLUES**

1.  Area around a house (6) 26 * 1 * 9 * 12 * 47 * 17

2.  Useful for wafting (3) 15 * 25 * 35

3.  Rich, affluent (7) 28 * 8 * 11 * 10 * 7 * 31 * 37

4.  Powers machines (4) 39 * 16 * 34 * 33

5.  Game played on court (6) 21* 27 * 5 * 24 * 29* 2

6.  A picture or painting of a person (8) 3 * 44 * 20 * 36 * 48 * 22 * 4 * 30

7.  The end of a pen or pencil (3) 40 * 23 * 32

8.  Shy (3) 18 * 14 * 13

9.  Glow brilliantly like gold (5) 6 * 46 * 41 * 45 * 19

10. Good-looking (8)
    49 * 50 * 51 * 52 * 53 * 38 * 42 * 43 *

| 1 | | 2 | 3 | 4 | 5 | 6 | 7 | 8 | 9 | |

| 10 | 11 | 12 | 13 | | 14 | 15 | |

| 16 | 17 | 18 | 19 | 20 | 21 | 22 | 23 | 24 | |

| 25 | 26 | 27 | | 28 | 29 | 30 | 31 | |

| 32 | 33 | 34 | 35 | 36 | 37 | | 38 | 39 | |

| 40 | 41 | 42 | 43 | | 44 | 45 | |

| 46 | 47 | 48 | | 49 | 50 | 51 | 52 | 53 | |

# GOSSIP

**Mrs Price-Ridley**, **Miss Hartnell** and **Miss Weatherby** do like to know what is happening at St Mary Mead. Like Miss Marple, their houses are close to the vicarage, and they pride themselves in keeping informed about the comings and goings. A few days before Colonel Protheroe's murder, Griselda Clement, the vicar's young wife, hosted her neighbours for tea at the vicarage.

'I couldn't help but notice that yesterday, Anne Protheroe called just before her daughter, Lettice,' smiled Miss Weatherby.

'I don't like to correct you,' said Mrs Price-Ridley, 'but Mary the housemaid appeared just after Anne.'

'If you recollect things properly, you must remember that Mary arrived before Anne, not after her,' Miss Hartnell added.

Unsurprisingly, the lists of the order in which the seven people entered the vicarage from the three ladies were not the same. They did agree that seven people called. The people were (in alphabetical order) **Anne Protheroe**, **Colonel Protheroe**, **Dennis Clement**, **Griselda Clement** (who had gone out earlier), **Lawrence Redding**, **Lettice Protheroe** and **Mary**, the housemaid. There was not a single individual that all three ladies had placed in the same order of arriving. However, each of the callers was correctly placed by at least one of the ladies. Each of the three ladies managed to put THREE callers in the correct order. From first to seventh, there was no instance where all the three ladies got the answer wrong.

**Can you work out the order that the visitors arrived at the vicarage?**

|  | First | Second | Third | Fourth | Fifth | Sixth | Seventh |
|---|---|---|---|---|---|---|---|
| Mrs Price-Ridley | Anne | Mary | Dennis | Lawrence | Lettice | Griselda | Colonel |
| Miss Hartnell | Dennis | Anne | Lawrence | Colonel | Mary | Lettice | Griselda |
| Miss Weatherby | Lawrence | Colonel | Mary | Anne | Lettice | Dennis | Griselda |

# HYMN NUMBERS

The vicar's wife, Griselda Clement, has chosen the hymns for the next Sunday service at the church in St Mary Mead. The order of the hymns follows a particular pattern, and Griselda has omitted the final one.

**Following the pattern, work out the number of the hymn which will end the service.**

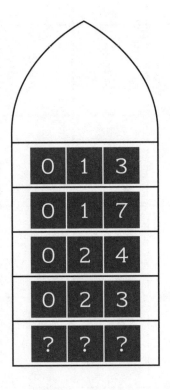

# WORD LADDER

Miss Marple deemed Inspector Slack to be 'rude and overbearing', but here we will use his name to create different words.

Start with the Inspector's name at the top of the ladder and arrive at a different word at the bottom. You must change one letter at a time and make a proper word with each move. Names of people or places must NOT be used — I will be checking . . .

| LADDER 1 | LADDER 2 |
|----------|----------|
| S L A C K | S L A C K |
| _ _ _ _ _ | _ _ _ _ _ |
| _ _ _ _ _ | _ _ _ _ _ |
| _ _ _ _ _ | _ _ _ _ _ |
| _ _ _ _ _ | _ _ _ _ _ |
| G U I D E | C H O R E |

# GRAVESTONES

It seems there have been quite a few murders in the village. **Do the inscriptions on the gravestones carry a clue as to how the unfortunate folk met their untimely demise?**

### 1
D I E
S P O O N

### 2
G R I N
D O W N

### 3
E D' S
M O T H E R

### 4
L E S T
G R A N D

### 5
G L U E D
O N  B E D

### 6
D O  E A T
C U F F S

### 7
B A D
B E S T

### 8
P A Y
D E A T H
S I X

# BEAT THE CLOCK

The clock in the vicarage study was always set fifteen minutes fast, which led to some confusion as to the time of death of Colonel Protheroe. Beat the clock with these timepiece teasers.

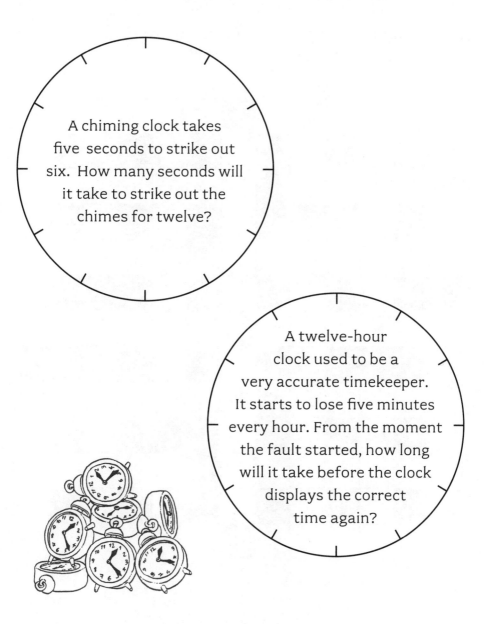

A chiming clock takes five seconds to strike out six. How many seconds will it take to strike out the chimes for twelve?

A twelve-hour clock used to be a very accurate timekeeper. It starts to lose five minutes every hour. From the moment the fault started, how long will it take before the clock displays the correct time again?

# DOUBLE CROSS

Miss Marple is adept at identifying a double crosser, working out who is betraying their conscience when, on the surface, they are seemingly trying to help.

Double clues lead to one answer. The two clues have different meanings but lead to the same word.

## ACROSS

1  A place of education *
A shoal of fish (6)

4  Mitigate, act as a go-
between * Bad mood or
extreme anger (6)

9  More scarce * More
lightly cooked (5)

10  Multiplies by three * High
voices in the church choir (7)

11  Flowering plant * Surname
of the activist who created
comfortable women's
underwear (7)

13  Speak * Complete, total (5)

14  Season * Jump suddenly
or rapidly (6)

15  Fruit or vegetables preserved
in vinegar and spices * An
unwelcome plight (6)

18  Porcelain * Country
associated with 12 down (5)

20  A straight line on a
curve * Diversion from a
previous set course (7)

22  Form in which a book is
published * Whole number
of copies of a newspaper (7)

23  A type of terrier * Mound
of rough stones (5)

24  Understand mentally *
Swallow and process food (6)

25  An accounts book * A
flat gravestone (6)

## DOWN

1 Clean thoroughly with a brush * Rough vegetation (5)
2 Place to anchor for a ship * Protect a wanted criminal (7)
3 Paddle * A rower (3)
5 Beheading or hanging * Carrying out a task (9)
6 Test project * Aviator (5)
7 Postpone for later * Self-restraint, reticence (7)
8 Begin * Sudden movement of surprise (5)
12 Oriental officials from 18 across * Small oranges (9)
14 Achieve a planned goal * Take over the throne from a previous monarch (7)

16 Safe custody * Retaining possession of (7)
17 A rock * A gem (5)
19 Sugary cake covering * Formation of frozen water on a sea-going vessel (5)
21 High male voice * General drift of a document or speech (5)
23 Tapering rod used in billiards * Signal for an actor to enter the stage (3)

# THE CURATE'S COLLECTION

Mrs Price-Ridley was most put out. Having put a one-pound note in the collection bag during an early morning service, it had been observed later that the highest note in the bag was worth ten shillings. This led to an investigation in which the unfortunate curate Mr Hawes was implicated.

There were twelve parishioners at the service.

............................................................................................

◯  Mrs Price-Ridley put £1 in the bag.

............................................................................................

◯  Two parishioners put in five shillings each and two more dropped in two half-crowns each.

............................................................................................

◯  Three parishioners put in twice the total of two half-crowns each.

............................................................................................

◯  One parishioner put in a ten-shilling note, one added four sixpences, and two put in a florin each.

**What was the total collection at the early morning service before the bag was taken away by the curate?**

Dear Aunt Mary,

I must thank you for your letter and expert
puzzle advice. I knew I could count on
you to unravel that difficult conundrum -
though why it appeared on Mrs Ashmore's
desk is still a mystery to me. Completing
the puzzle bundle has been my priority,
since I cannot find its author. With
no one in the house able to tell me
where Mrs Ashmore may be, I have begun
to investigate myself.

I examined the corkboard above Mrs
Ashmore's desk, seeing notices from the
local church. I have heard that the local
vicar is as abrasive as Agatha Christie's
Colonel Protheroe, but cannot imagine
that a librarian such as Mrs Ashmore is
embroiled in anything untoward here at
the house.

My eyes wandered to the shelf next to the
corkboard, where a large potted plant looked
like it had recently been moved, its soil
spilling onto the floor below. The knotgrass
flowering inside was itself a strange choice
for indoor growing, but even more surprising
was the small paperback copy of *The Murder
at the Vicarage* I found shoved to the bottom
of the pot.

The sheaf of papers sticking out looked faintly familiar, and so I have my second bundle of puzzles to be solved. Is Mrs Ashmore leaving me my very own cryptic messages? I am beginning to decipher them and feel a similar amount of vexation at another of her puzzles, which I share with you below.

Where could Mrs Ashmore be and what might have befallen her?

Your nephew,

Charles

# DOING THE ROUNDS

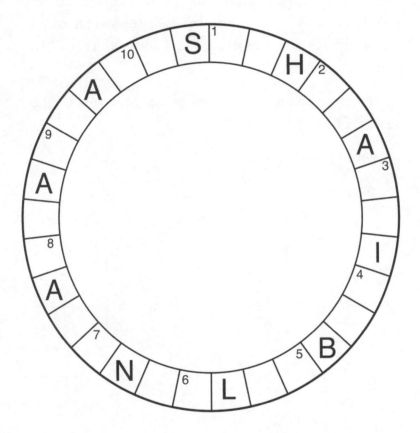

The completed circle above will contain ten
words of five letters. Each word starts in
a numbered space and reads clockwise. Words
overlap, so the last two letters of one word
become the first two of the next.

All the middle letters are in place, so use
the pairs of letters to form the words.

Be careful, as there is a pair of letters
below that are a red herring, so keep alert
as you're deciphering.

CH  ER  ET  FE  IN

LY  RA  SE  ST  TO  ZE

# CHAPTER 3

# 4.50 from Paddington

# POINTS EAST

Below are sections of track and points. In each of the six puzzles, there are words going east from the points.

**1.**

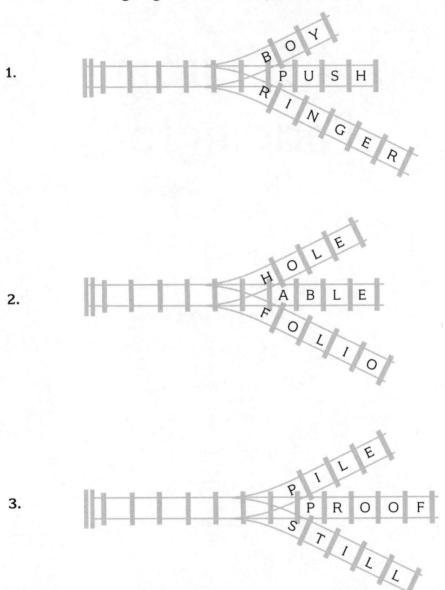

Which railway word can go in front of the words in each example to make new ones?

4.

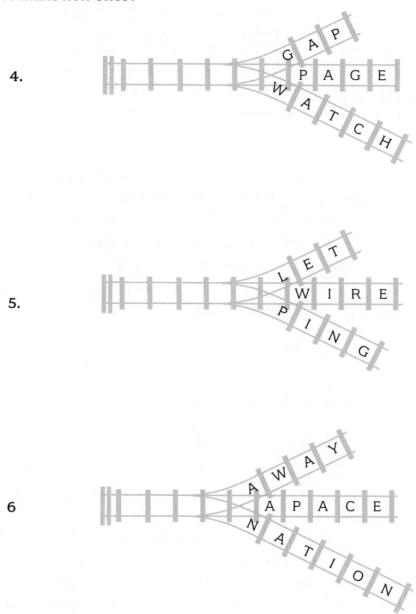

G A P

P A G E

W A T C H

5.

L E T

W I R E

P I N G

6

A W A Y

A P A C E

N A T I O N

# THE CARRIAGE MURDER

| A1 | A2 | A3 | A4 | A5 | A6 | A7 |
|----|----|----|----|----|----|----|

| GATE A | PLATFORM |
|--------|----------|

Mrs McGillicuddy was convinced that she witnessed a woman being strangled in the carriage of an adjacent train. Our train has seven first-class carriages. There is no connecting corridor. Each carriage has a number on the door from A1 to A7. A1 is nearest to the gate as passengers enter the platform. One of the carriages was occupied by a gentleman and a lady. That is where the murder took place. **Which one is it?**

## CLUES

Each carriage has a number on the door from A1 to A7.

Reverend Batty was on the train. He was in a carriage on his own. 'I'll tell you something odd,' he said quietly. 'The number of my carriage . . . that was an odd number. Damned if I can remember what it was, though.'

Lady Pearl was on her own. She confirmed that she looked in the windows either side of the carriage she finally chose. There was a gentleman in both carriages, but she could not say if anyone else was with them.

Colonel Upshot said: 'I walked down the platform and saw that Batty was alone in a carriage. Batty by name and batty by nature. The chap always starts singing hymns! Shared a carriage with him once and had to listen to "Onward, Christian Soldiers" three times on the journey. Didn't want to be either side of him. He's got such a loud voice! I carried on down the platform and made sure there were two carriages between us. As it turned out, there was a group of women gabbling away at one side of me and two people arguing on the other side of me.'

A group of eight ladies were returning from a shopping trip. They had wanted to split into two groups of four and have adjacent carriages, but that wasn't possible. 'We could not have been further apart in the first-class section if we had tried,' sniffed one of the ladies.

Miss Piggot, a governess, almost missed the train. She rushed into the nearest empty carriage from the gate. 'I wish I hadn't done that,' she confessed. 'There was some awful man in the next carriage singing hymns! I wouldn't mind, but he was a semi-tone flat.'

# SEARCHING FOR SUSTENANCE

Lucy Eyelesbarrow is Rutherford Hall's very own domestic goddess. She breezes through household chores and is also an excellent cook. Young Alexander and pal James, home for the school holidays, are particular fans of her culinary skills. In the word search grid there are the names of many of their favourite foods. Words appear as a straight line of letters that can read across, back, up, down or diagonally.

When you have finished finding them, look for unused letters. Go clockwise along the top line, down the right-hand column, right to left across the bottom, and up the left hand column. You'll produce something the family at Rutherford Hall made famous.

APPLE MERINGUE
BACON
BAKED CUSTARD
BISCUITS
BUTTER
CAKE
CANAPÉS
CHEESE
CHICKEN
CHIPS
CHUTNEY
CURRY
EGGS
FISH PASTE
GRAVY

MILK
MUSHROOMS
POTATOES
RICE
ROAST BEEF
SANDWICHES
SOUP
SPANISH OMELETTE
STEAK
SYLLABUB
TEAS
TREACLE TART
VEGETABLES
WINE

```
B C C V B C F I S H P A S T E
A X H U E A T Y L S Q U S T R
K P I I J G C H E E S E T R A
E Z P L C E E O J U D E I E C
D M S L R K T T N R L V U A H
C S U X E A E K A E T S C C U
U E R S T M T N M B R H S L T
S P I O H E E O C I L Y I E N
T A P Y A R H R C T L E B T E
A N V S E S O E I L E K S A Y
R A L T I O T O A N G A L R V
D C T N E U G B M R G C R T A
S U A T N P U W E S S U A T R
B P Q U I B U O H E C V E P G
S A N D W I C H E S F R E K C
```

# FESTIVE SYMBOLS

Members of the Crackenthorpe family had been home for Christmas. Alex and his friend James had enjoyed hospitality at Rutherford Hall during their school holidays. In this puzzle, letters in the names of favourite Christmas decorations have been replaced by symbols. The answer to **clue 1** is **BELLS**. Continue and deck Rutherford Hall for the festive season, if you have the smarts.

**CLUES**

1. ○ ✳ ▲ ▲ ◎

2. ○ □ ◇ ○ ▲ ✳ ◎

3. □ ◪ △ ✳ ▲

4. ● ◐ ◩ ◎ ✳ ▲

5. ● ■ ✳ ✳

6. ◸ □ ■ ▲ □ ◪ ▼

7. ▲ ◐ △ ⦚ ● ◎

8. ⊞ □ ⊞ ✳ ■ ⊟ ⦚ □ ◐ ◪ ◎

# STATION-ARY

Here is a map of railway lines and rural stations close by Milchester. **Your task is to plot a route that will call at as many stations as possible, without revisiting a piece of track or going over a crossing point more than once.** It is NOT possible to visit them all! Go from the arrow top left to the arrow top right.

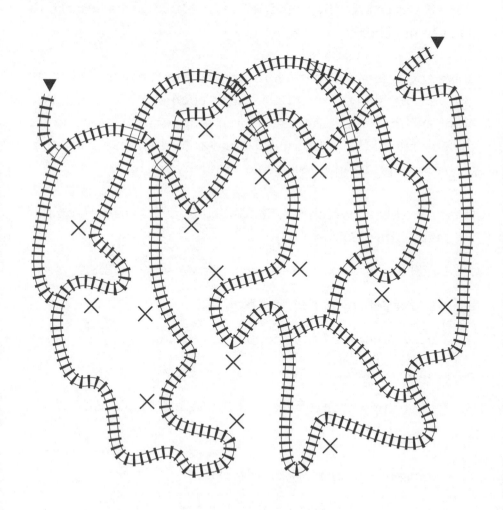

# MISS MARPLE PRESCRIBES

Mrs Elspeth McGillicuddy is convinced she has witnessed a murder on the train from London, whilst she is on her way to visit her great friend Miss Jane Marple. **Clearly Mrs McGillicuddy is in some distress after her experience, so Miss Marple prescribes what to help her?**

Solve the clues and write your answers in the larger grid. All answers have eight letters. Next to each clue 1 to 9 are two numbers. In clue 10, there are three numbers. These stand for the position of the letters in the answer. Write these in order in the smaller grid and Miss Marple's remedy will be revealed.

1.  A periodical, which Mrs McGillicuddy was reading on her memorable journey (2.3)

2.  Small towns or hamlets, such as St Mary Mead (3.5)

3.  Tool for cutting paper or thread (4.5)

4.  Thrown over the happy couple at weddings (2.4)

5.  A dark hard wood (1.8)

6.  Person appointed to carry out the bequests in a will (4.7)

7.  A radio (1.7)

8.  Spells away from work or school (3.4)

9.  Strong, having a great deal of influence (1.3)

10. A china or porcelain ornament depicting a person (2.7.8)

# SPOKES

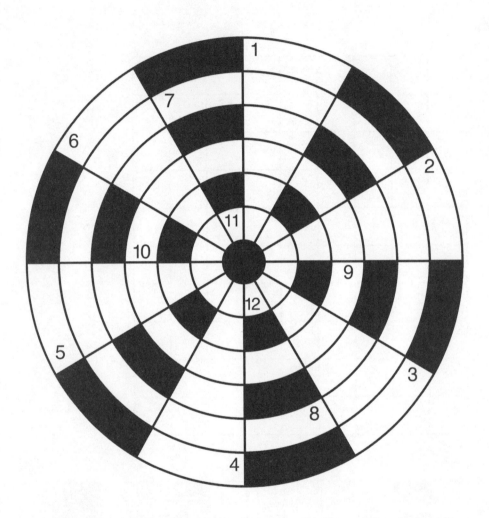

All answers have six letters and slot into the railway wheel. Some form the spokes and go from the outer edge of the wheel to the centre. Some are radial and go round the wheel in a clockwise direction.

1. Contents of a compact belonging to the first victim

2. Toxic substance such as arsenic

3. Utensil for heating water in the kitchen

4. A cosmetic

5. Luther's son who was a banker in London

6. Dermot Craddock is a member of this force

7. To flatter and persuade, as Lucy and Emma had to do with the older Mr Crackenthorpe

8. A vegetable, which Luther accused Lucy of using too much of

9. An artist's workplace, as might be used by Cedric

10. Those who hoard wealth and don't spend their money; Luther was a perfect example

11. A type of cake

12. Appliance to keep food cool, which Mrs Kidder said was unsafe

# UNCOUPLING

Locomotives and carriages are often coupling and uncoupling to make best use of the vehicles on the railway network and maintain good links. In this puzzle, you have to find a link between the two clue words and slot the correct answer in the grid.

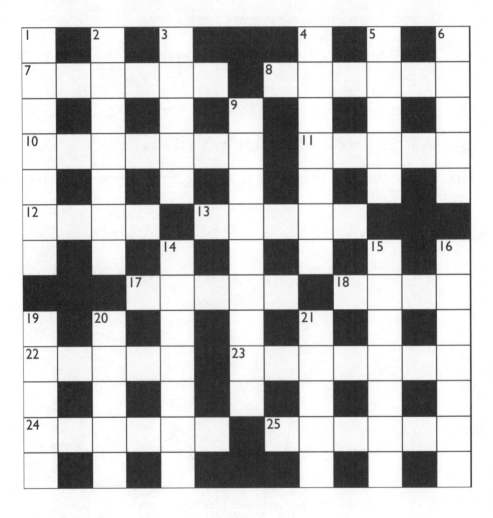

## ACROSS

7   Wild * Kingdom (6)
8   Beer * Organ (6)
10  Prison * Out (7)
11  Hand * Point (5)
12  Flower * Guide (4)
13  Table * Basket (5)
17  Dish * Cap (5)
18  Horse * String (4)
22  Stop * Gang (5)
23  Bank * Holder (7)
24  Red * Slippers (6)
25  Step * Figure (6)

## DOWN

1   German * Roll (7)
2   Public * Book (7)
3   Birthday * Line (5)
4   Cow * Sauce (7)
5   Clotted * Teas (5)
6   Land * Rule (5)
9   Merry * Pudding (9)
14  Sticking * Cast (7)
15  After * Provoking (7)
16  Love * Patent (7)
19  Outer * Ship (5)
20  Sweet * Ache (5)
21  Pacific * Liner (5)

# TIMETABLE

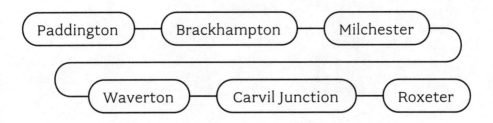

Paddington — Brackhampton — Milchester

Waverton — Carvil Junction — Roxeter

Rail users are travelling first class on the 4.50 from Paddington. There are twice as many gentlemen as ladies.

One lady and five gentlemen get out at the first stop. Three ladies board the train, but no gentlemen.

There are twice as many ladies in first class as gentlemen when the train pulls into Milchester. No one boards the train.

Surprisingly, no one gets on or off at Waverton.

There are the same number of passengers in first class on arrival at Roxeter as on leaving Paddington. Three ladies and three gentlemen travelled the entire route from Paddington to Roxeter.

**What was the movement of passengers in first class at Carvil Junction?**

# BACK ON TRACK

On a train, the locomotive and carriages are joined together and separated as needed.

In this puzzle, five examples of vehicles used on the railways, which have NINE letters in their names, have been separated into sections of three letters. The sections have become completely muddled up.

**Can you get things back on track and put the words back together again?**

| C | O | A |
|---|---|---|

| L | C | O |
|---|---|---|

| M | A | I |
|---|---|---|

| M | I | L |
|---|---|---|

| C | A | R |
|---|---|---|

| I | N | G |
|---|---|---|

| G | U | A |
|---|---|---|

| D | I | N |
|---|---|---|

| A | C | H |
|---|---|---|

| U | C | K |
|---|---|---|

| A | I | N |
|---|---|---|

| V | A | N |
|---|---|---|

| L | T | R |
|---|---|---|

| R | D | S |
|---|---|---|

| K | T | R |
|---|---|---|

Dear Aunt Mary,

You taught me to love a mystery. To enjoy the difficulty of discovery, to be entertained rather than give in to frustration. It is thanks to you that I was so encouraged to become the librarian here at Greenway, to look after the finest collection of mystery stories in the world.

I remind myself of this as I try not to let the mystery of my own days overwhelm me.

I still have yet to lay eyes on Mrs Ashmore. The only trace of her that remains are the puzzles I find, seemingly around every corner. The house manager tells me this is not an irregular occurrence, that Mrs Ashmore was often seen scribbling notes to herself to while away the time. She also told me that Mrs Ashmore is *usually* incredibly punctual, and even goes out of her way to arrive at all meetings and events agonisingly early. Why she has left me to fend for myself, I do not know.

As I paced the library floor in front of the window this afternoon, trying to make sense of it all, the afternoon sun shone on a large suitcase underneath the desk. I found no identifying documents inside, instead being greeted with a pristine copy of *4.50 from Paddington*. And what did I find within, but a little bunch of papers, which by now I recognised as puzzles expertly prepared by Mrs Ashmore.

I sat down at my desk to examine them and, as usual, they offered a stimulating challenge. Before I move on, I must beg your help with a particularly tough one I alone could not crack.

I will get to the bottom of this.

Your nephew,

Charles

# RETURN JOURNEY

Follow Mrs McGillicuddy's memorable railway
journey from Paddington into the English
countryside. Words linked to railways fill
the grid and read either across or down.
There is only one way to fit all the words.
Have a good journey ...

| 3 LETTERS | 6 LETTERS | 11 LETTERS |
|-----------|-----------|------------|
| ASK | BUFFET | LOCOMOTIVES |
| BAG | CLOCKS | |
| CAB | SCENIC | 12 LETTERS |
| EAT | SINGLE | REFRESHMENTS |
| MAP | TENDER | RETURN TICKET |
| RUN | | |
| SIT | 7 LETTERS | 13 LETTERS |
| TEA | BARRIER | BOOKING |
| USE | BUFFERS | OFFICE |
| | ENGINES | |
| 4 LETTERS | NON STOP | 14 LETTERS |
| BUSY | PASSAGE | PASSENGER |
| HELP | STATION | TRAIN |
| MAIL | TOURIST | |
| MEET | WHISTLE | 15 LETTERS |
| SEAT | | RAILWAY |
| SIGN | 8 LETTERS | CARRIAGE |
| WAIT | CORRIDOR | |
| | SLEEPERS | |
| 5 LETTERS | | |
| AISLE | 9 LETTERS | |
| ROUTE | DEPARTURE | |
| SERVE | DINING CAR | |
| STEER | | |
| TRACK | 10 LETTERS | |
| | FIRST CLASS | |
| | TRAIN LINES | |

# CHAPTER 4

# A Murder Is Announced

# CRYPTIC

You will know that *A Murder Is Announced* opens with a cryptic message about an invitation to a murder. In this puzzle, cryptic clues lead to solutions in the crossword grid. As with all good mysteries, nothing is as it seems.

## ACROSS

1 Chased around to pay in cheque (6)

4 These are not stable in the dining room (6)

9 In diagrams apparently where the Colonel came from (5)

10 Deals with what Handel's rewritten (7)

11 Piece in the Gazette about new recital (7)

13 Revelation is unclear in part concerning relative (5)

14 Painful experience which you will reload in a different way (6)

15 Hit the goal the coders decipher (6)

18 Christmas song for this girl (5)

20 One of several little ones where Letitia lived? (7)

22 Well adjusted Pat dead, in this way (7)

23 Broken plate shows part of a violet (5)

24 Mid Med sadly has lost some light (6)

25 Sparse alteration shows what's left over (6)

## DOWN

1 Chain smashed in what the shepherdess figurine was made from (5)

2 Dead set on procuring induced sleep (7)

3 Are changes coming in this period? (3)

5 Made public, ad nun once edited (9)

6 Cilla turns a shade of purple! (5)

7 Defer point up ends in order (7)

8 Screw up fiche for the one in charge (5)

12 Apple dish for a Blacklock sister? (8)

14 Fruit trees or chard being harvested (7)

16 Store or distribute in Amy Murgatroyd's hen coop (7)

17 His pa definitely finds the garden tool (5)

19 Real moment reveals kingdom (5)

21 Murders with strange skill (5)

23 Phillipa briefly makes high pitched signal (3)

# THE ANNOUNCEMENT

---

*'A murder is announced and will take place on
Friday, October 29th,
at Little Paddocks at 6.30 p.m.
Friends please accept this, the only intimation.'*

---

This notice in the pages of the *North Benham News* and *Chipping Cleghorn Gazette* certainly caught the attention of the villagers. Was it a silly joke? Was it some sort of game? Was there a possibility that something sinister was going to happen?

**Can you work out what is going on in the similar notices opposite?**

## A

'It is announced that on Friday, October 29th, at Little Paddocks at 6.30 p.m. a visitor will arrive who has been around countless centuries, but never survived longer than a month. Friends please accept this, the only intimation.'

## B

'A crime is announced and will take place on Friday, October 29th, at Little Paddocks at 6.30 p.m. when something precious will be shattered in the room. Friends please accept this, the only intimation.'

## C

'A murder trial is announced and will take place on Friday, October 29th, at Little Paddocks at 6.30 p.m. It will be revealed which word is always spelt inaccurately at murder trials. Friends please accept this, the only intimation.'

## D

'The answer to a murderous conundrum will be announced on Friday, October 29th, at Little Paddocks at 6.30 p.m. The person who made it, made it for someone else. The person who bought it didn't need it. The person who got it didn't know that it was theirs. What was it? Friends please accept this, the only intimation.'

# SWITCHED IDENTITY

Several characters in *A Murder Is Announced* are living under an assumed name. They are not who they seem.

The words listed opposite will switch identity as well. Identify the anagram of the listed words in the grid. Answers are in straight lines and go across, backwards, up, down and diagonally. Be careful, some starter words are anagrams of more than one word . . .

| Q | U | E | S | A | E | S | I | D | H | S | N | O | O | P |
|---|---|---|---|---|---|---|---|---|---|---|---|---|---|---|
| U | A | G | R | N | I | T | H | M | O | T | S | E | S | I |
| L | T | I | J | S | O | R | C | O | U | V | A | H | D | S |
| H | E | T | R | W | G | E | I | U | O | R | O | E | L | T |
| H | X | A | T | E | O | V | A | S | E | T | D | L | D | O |
| I | O | I | D | R | L | D | I | V | J | O | I | E | Z | L |
| R | M | L | C | S | R | A | L | O | C | K | S | N | R | Y |
| E | O | I | H | E | C | I | T | A | L | S | I | P | G | O |
| L | E | O | U | G | S | N | S | I | D | E | A | U | N | T |
| A | J | Y | M | O | A | E | Z | N | O | R | T | S | I | P |
| T | E | L | L | E | T | R | E | S | T | N | H | S | T | L |
| I | D | V | G | A | L | I | D | P | E | A | R | L | T | D |
| V | E | R | T | E | R | P | O | E | A | L | E | Z | E | O |
| E | E | S | O | F | L | Y | Z | C | N | M | A | O | S | R |
| S | E | H | C | R | O | T | A | T | R | E | T | S | I | S |

| | |
|---|---|
| ACES | PART |
| DALES | PECTINS |
| DANGER | RAWNESS |
| ESTRANGE | RED RUM |
| FINDERS | RESIST |
| HATED | SAVE |
| HATTER | SEASIDE |
| HECTORS | SKILL |
| HIRE | SLIVER |
| HOST | SOOTHING |
| ITEM | SPOILT |
| LOVES | SPOON |
| MOOR | STARVED |
| MUCH | TEA SET |
| OLIVETS | TESTING |
| ORIENTAL | TUNA |
| PALER | VERSATILE |

# SEPARATED

Pip and Emma are twins who lived separate lives. In this puzzle, it is the words that have become separated and need to join together again. Look at each word in column A and match each one up with a word in column B, so that a new word is created.

| COLUMN A | COLUMN B |
|----------|----------|
| ASP | ACHE |
| BAN | AGE |
| BAND | IRE |
| CAP | KING |
| CUT | LASS |
| IMP | PARTS |
| PAN | PORT |
| PAT | RIOT |
| RAM | ROVE |
| SUP | SIZE |

# RATIONING

From the outbreak of World War II in 1939 until the end of the war in 1945, food and other commodities were rationed. Here, the names of some of those rationed items have been written in code. Each letter of the alphabet has been replaced by a number.

**If SUGAR is written as 1. 2. 3. 4. 5. what are these items?**

**A**   6. 3. 3. 1.

**B**   7. 6. 4.

**C**   8. 6. 4. 7.

**D**   9. 2. 7. 7. 6. 5.

**E**   8. 4. 5. 3. 4. 5. 10. 11. 6.

**F**   1. 12. 6. 6. 7. 1.

**G**   13. 2. 5. 5. 4. 11. 7. 1.

**H**   13. 14. 6. 6. 1. 6.

# NEGATIVE

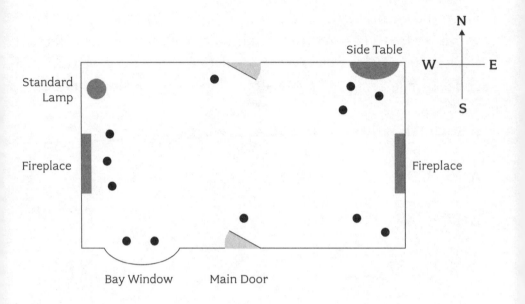

Twelve people have gathered in a drawing room, summoned by a puzzling message. The lights go out and confusion ensues.

People inevitably move about before the lights come back on again. **Where was everyone when the lights went out?** Match names to the positions indicated in the sketch.

The twelve guests are: Alice, Bryan, Colin, Dorothy, Edward, Fiona, Gerald, Hattie, Iris, June, Keith and Leonard.

## CLUES

**Iris said:** 'I definitely wasn't in the eastern half of the room. I was trying to find Leonard, but he hid in a corner somewhere. I wasn't by the bay window.'

**Alice said:** 'One of the gentlemen stood on his own near the main door. He had his back to me and was looking towards the front door. He looked too small to be Colin. I don't remember who was near me, but I wasn't far from the door on the north side of the room.'

**June said:** 'Two men were in a corner of the room, to the right of the fireplace, and had been laughing about some silly joke. I am sure that neither Colin nor Edward were in the group.'

**Hattie said:** 'I am sure that I was the person nearest the standard lamp. In fact, I backed into it. That was bad enough, but when I turned round I apologised, thinking I had pushed into someone else.'

**Dorothy said:** 'I noticed that there were two groups of three people, both made up of a gentleman and two ladies. Well, I say gentleman! Bryan invited me here, but straight away he left me. He couldn't get much further away from me.'

**Gerald said:** 'I wasn't in the western half of the room, but Colin was. I know I was talking to someone whose name I can never remember.'

No one in the room has a person either side of them with a name beginning with the next letter in the alphabet to them.

# PRAISE INDEED

Solve the clues and write your answers in the larger grid. All answers have EIGHT letters. Take the keycoded letters and put them in their correct places in the smaller grid to spell out a quotation.

One of the characters in *A Murder Is Announced* gives an opinion on another. The quote begins, 'She's just . . .' Take the letters in the shaded squares left to right, top to bottom to spell out the surname of the character who hands out this high praise.

1. The Yard, which is the HQ of the Metropolitan Police

2. Of great worth, such as precious gems or paintings

3. Limited to a certain amount, such as with food and fuel during the war years

4. Who someone is, their personality or individuality

5. Person who looks after sheep, as portrayed on Miss Blacklock's figurine

6. Killed with strychnine or arsenic, for example

7. A small firearm

8. A pseudonym, often an affectionate one, such as 'Bunny' for Dora Bunner

9. Someone who looks after the flowers and trees around a house, such as Phillipa Haymes

10. Those who have fled persecution in their homeland, housekeeper Mitzi, for example

| | A | B | C | D | E | F | G | H |
|---|---|---|---|---|---|---|---|---|
| 1 | | | | | | | | |
| 2 | | | | | | | | |
| 3 | | | | | | | | |
| 4 | | | | | | | | |
| 5 | | | | | | | | |
| 6 | | | | | | | | |
| 7 | | | | | | | | |
| 8 | | | | | | | | |
| 9 | | | | | | | | |
| 10 | | | | | | | | |

| D1 | B5 | H2 | | C10 | F4 | F3 | B7 | D6 | E4 | | | | |
|---|---|---|---|---|---|---|---|---|---|---|---|---|---|
| | | | | | | | | | | | | | |
| D9 | G3 | C3 | H8 | C8 | G4 | C6 | F7 | G10 | | A9 | C1 | H5 | |
| | | | | | | | | | | | | | |
| C5 | C7 | G9 | A10 | | G8 | B2 | H6 | E9 | | | | | |
| | | | | | | | | | | | | | |

# FLY THE FLAG

Europe features heavily in *A Murder Is Announced*. Rudi was Swiss, Mitzi was a refugee from Europe, and we are told Phillipa's husband died in Italy during the war.

Answer the questions opposite, which have a European flavour, and write the answers starting in the numbered square downwards. When the grid is complete, the shaded horizontal row will spell out the name of somewhere in Europe.

| 1 | 2 | 3 | 4 | 5 | 6 | 7 | 8 | 9 | 10 | 11 |
|---|---|---|---|---|---|---|---|---|----|----|
|   |   |   |   |   |   |   |   |   |    |    |
|   |   |   |   |   |   |   |   |   |    |    |
|   |   |   |   |   |   |   |   |   |    |    |
|   |   |   |   |   |   |   |   |   |    |    |
|   |   |   |   |   |   |   |   |   |    |    |
|   |   |   |   |   |   |   |   |   |    |    |
|   |   |   |   |   |   |   |   |   |    |    |

1. It divides England from France

2. Swiss lake

3. Country, capital Vienna

4. National ones are sung at sporting and formal events

5. Gorgonzola, Gouda and Pecorino are examples of these

6. Country on the eastern shore of the Black Sea

7. Island, with active volcanoes, just south of the Arctic Circle

8. Composer of waltzes who came from clue 3

9. You are this nationality if you hail from Barcelona

10. Flat-bottomed boat seen on the canals of Venice

11. A native of Moscow or St Petersburg

# DELICIOUS DEATH

Delicious Death was the name given to a rich and intense chocolate cake made by Miss Blacklock's housekeeper, Mitzi. Mitzi's recipe was a closely guarded secret, but you will find links to the speciality in the puzzle below.

Words fit back into the grid and read across or down. There is only one possible solution. **One ingredient has been missed out. What is it?**

## 3 LETTERS

DRY
ICE
JAR
PAN
RUM

## 4 LETTERS

BAKE
EGGS
FORK
OVEN
PIPE
RICH
STIR
TINS
TRAY

## 5 LETTERS

BOWLS
SERVE
SPOON
SWEET
TASTE
WHISK

## 6 LETTERS

BASINS
BRANDY
BUTTER
RECIPE
SPREAD

## 7 LETTERS

FILLING
PERFECT
RAISINS
VANILLA

## 8 LETTERS

CHERRIES
DECORATE

## 10 LETTERS

APRICOT JAM
BROWN SUGAR

## 11 LETTERS

DOUBLE CREAM

## 12 LETTERS

BAKING POWDER
FLOWER PETALS

## 13 LETTERS

DARK CHOCOLATE
GROUND ALMONDS

## 18 LETTERS

CRYSTALLIZED GINGER

# NAME CHECK

Each group of letters below can be completed with the letters in the name of a character from *A Murder Is Announced*. The letters might not be next to each other, but they are always in the same order as they are in the name . . .

---

**1.**    I N F _ _ _

_ _ E T H _ S T

W _ R _ L _

---

**2.**    E _ _ _ _ T E

P _ _ _ E N T _ A L

_ _ _ _ M E N T A R Y

---

**3.**    A _ _ _ _ B L E

_ _ _ M _ N T

_ E C _ _ _ T E D

---

**4.** B A G _ _ _ E S

_ A R S N _ _

E _ _ T A _ H

**5.** _ _ S M I _ _

_ _ C K K _ I F _

_ _ U _ D I C _

Dear Aunt Mary,

While I still have no news from Mrs Ashmore,
I am getting used to this mysterious state
of affairs. I have set about answering
letters addressed to her, learning the
filing system and trying my very best to get
to grips with my new role.

I was interrupted from my tasks this
morning, however, to receive the most
peculiar piece of post. Hand-delivered by
the local postman was a rather expensive-
looking string of pearls Mrs Ashmore had
recently been convinced to order, alongside
an envelope with only the words 'For the
librarian' typed on the front.

It included a copy of *A Murder Is
Announced*, signed with Mrs Ashmore's name.
A new bundle of puzzles was safely tucked
inside for me. Forgive me, but I do see them
as mine now, so I have taken possession of
them. I certainly see them as my personal
responsibility to complete.

This mystery grows ever more complex as
each day passes, and I grow more certain I
shan't ever meet Mrs Ashmore.

Please, do write back, dear aunt. I am in
need of your advice.

Your nephew,

Charles

# HONEY POT

The villagers of Chipping Cleghorn often swap items among themselves, especially if there is a glut of homegrown produce. In the honeycomb grid, answers are written in the hexagonal squares and can go clockwise or anticlockwise around the number. It's up to you to work out the direction. All answers have SIX letters.

The first letter of the first answer starts in the hexagon top right of number 1, and begins with M.

1. The black one might involve illicit traffic of goods

2. Colonel Easterbrook, to family and friends

3. A necklace, which hopefully wouldn't have this effect

4. Rescind or withdraw a will

5. Describes a formal jacket for evening wear

6. Ask guests to attend a function where clue 5 might be worn

7. Person exposed to gunfire

8. Where Phillipa works

9. Draw a logical conclusion

10. Messrs Craddock, Rydesdale and formerly Clithering collectively

11. Those long absent from their native land

12. Assets and liabilities after death

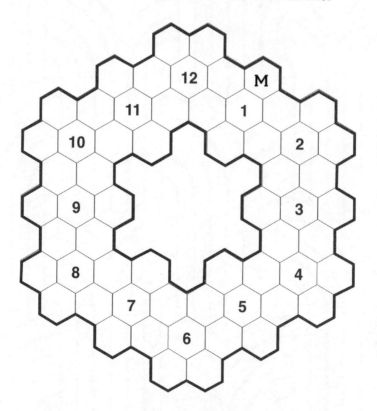

# CHAPTER 5

# The ABC Murders

# ALPHA CODE

Each letter of the alphabet is represented by a number from 1 to 26.

I will be kind and give you the numbers which represent the letters in **DEVON**, the home county of victim number three of *The ABC Murders*, to start you off. So, every space with a **1** in it contains a D, every **2** is an E, every **3** is a V, every **4** is an O and every **5** is an N. Try to complete the grid where words read either across or down.

| | 11 | | 2 | | 1 | | | 14 | | 6 | | 13 | |
|---|---|---|---|---|---|---|---|---|---|---|---|---|---|
| 23 | 7 | 11 | 26 | 2 | 17 | | 15 | 20 | 2 | 6 | 9 | 8 | 4 | 5 |
| | 8 | | 2 | | 4 | | | 9 | | 7 | | 13 | |
| 6 | 9 | 7 | 12 | | 3 | 4 | 8 | 10 | 2 | | 9 | 8 | 2 | 1 |
| | 17 | | 17 | | 2 | | 5 | | | 8 | | 5 | |
| 1 | 2 | 3 | 4 | 5 | | 4 | 3 | 2 | 17 | 10 | 4 | 7 | 9 | 6 |
| | D | E | V | O | N | | | | | | | | |
| | 6 | | 11 | | 16 | | 8 | | 4 | | 5 | | |
| | 6 | | | 9 | 2 | 7 | 6 | 18 | 4 | 25 | | | 1 |
| | 2 | | | 7 | | 8 | | 13 | | 5 | | 4 | |
| 25 | 7 | 6 | 6 | 2 | 17 | 6 | 12 | 26 | | 17 | 7 | 21 | 4 | 17 |
| | 17 | | 10 | | | 23 | | 6 | | 17 | | 17 | |
| 7 | 17 | 2 | 7 | | 2 | 19 | 2 | 10 | 9 | | 17 | 4 | 12 | 6 |
| | 2 | | 25 | | 22 | | | 4 | | 7 | | 2 | |
| 7 | 6 | 9 | 2 | 17 | 8 | 6 | 24 | | 23 | 8 | 9 | 9 | 23 | 2 |
| | 9 | | 1 | | 9 | | | 2 | | 2 | | 23 | |

The checklist below will help to keep track of the letters you have found.

| 1. D | 2. E | 3. V | 4. O | 5. N | 6. | 7. | 8. | 9. | 10. | 11. | 12. | 13. |
|---|---|---|---|---|---|---|---|---|---|---|---|---|
| 14. | 15. | 16. | 17. | 18. | 19. | 20. | 21. | 22. | 23. | 24. | 25. | 26. |

When you have filled in the crossword and worked out what all the letters stand for, look at the numbers below.

**Can you work out the name of a toy, which Poirot likens to an investigation?**

# 19. 8. 16. 6. 7. 11.

— — — — — —

# LAST LIST

**ANDOVER, BEXHILL-ON-SEA, CHURSTON** and **DONCASTER.**

These are the FIRST four locations in the alphabetical list in *The ABC Murders*. Where would the next locations have been, if Poirot had not caught the murderer? Here are some possible locations for **E** to **M**.

The letters in the names have been moved around and the places are NOT listed in alphabetical order. Good hunting!

1. TUTOR AGA RHYME (two words)

2. LIMB FOR ACE

3. HAVE FARMS

4. TRUE AS BONE

5. KENT TIGER

6. SAD NO TIME

7. ANCESTRAL

8. OR HATE RAG

9. RAJ ROW

# TRUE TO TYPE

Which portable typewriter from the 1930s produced this message? Each typewriter has its own quirks and foibles . . . enough to provide evidence to identify the machine used to send the message, if you're smart enough.

```
Where will  the next murder take  place?
You will have to wait for my next letter
to find out. I  think that a day by the sea
            might be fun!
```

......................................................................................

**Typewriter 1**
In poor condition. Space bar is not always consistently accurate. The return key to create new lines is totally unreliable.

......................................................................................

**Typewriter 2**
Generally in good condition. The ribbon is worn and some letters can appear quite faint. The keys d and e have been overworked and never print cleanly. Space bar leaves some double spacing.

......................................................................................

**Typewriter 3**
Generally in good condition. The space bar is quite stiff and occasionally produces a double space. A couple of letters appear to be quite faint, but this is not consistent.

......................................................................................

**Typewriter 4**
Generally in good condition. Occasional faintness in the letter e. Capital letters do not sit on the line.

# GONE MISSING

The letters **A B C** remain in these words but all other letters have been removed. Can you complete the words with the other letters?

1.  It covers an item of dining furniture in a tea room

    _ A B _ _ C _ _ _ _

2.  Relating to a condition where there is too much sugar in the blood

    _ _ A B _ _ _ C

3.  Woven material or textile

    _ A B _ _ C

4.  Leave unlawfully to avoid arrest

    A B _ C _ _ _

5.  The kidnap or removal of a person by force or deceit

    A B _ _ C _ _ _ _

6.  An official barrier in a thoroughfare to stop traffic

    _ _ A _ B _ _ C _

7.  The refraining from food or alcohol

    A B _ _ _ _ _ _ C _

8.  The proverb says it makes the heart grow fonder

    A B _ _ _ C _

# NINE LIVES

Solve the clues below and write your answers in the correct boxes in the grid. When the nine letters are in place, you will have discovered a name connected with *The ABC Murders*.

| 1 | 2 | 3 | 4 | 5 | 6 | 7 | 8 | 9 |
|---|---|---|---|---|---|---|---|---|
|   |   |   |   |   |   |   |   |   |

## CLUES

1.  A feline, part of the name of the café where Betty Barnard worked

    4   5   7

2.  The crime of betraying one's country

    7   9   8   5   6   2   3

3.  A cipher, which may use the letters ABC

    4   2   1   8

# WORD PLAY

Answer the clue questions and slot them into their correct places reading across in the larger grid. All answers have **SEVEN** letters.

When this grid is complete, take the letters in the keycoded squares and write them in the smaller grid. For example, B2 is the first reference for the smaller grid. Using the larger grid move down column B and across in row 2. The letter in the square that matches both column and row reference is a T, and that transfers to the smaller grid.

When the smaller grid is complete, the words will reveal a quotation by Hercule Poirot, from *The ABC Murders*.

The quotation begins, 'Words, mademoiselle, are only . . .'

1. Suitcases, bags etc. which you take on a journey

2. Where a train stops

3. Communications which arrive via the post

4. Male sibling, such as Carmichael or Franklin Clarke

5. A coastal resort like Bexhill, for example

6. A document, which is not genuine, a counterfeit

7. Talk quickly, and maybe indiscreetly or about nothing in particular

8. Horse-drawn carriages, comfortable single-decker buses, or railway carriages

|   | A | B | C | D | E | F | G |
|---|---|---|---|---|---|---|---|
| 1 |   |   |   |   |   |   |   |
| 2 |   | T |   |   |   |   |   |
| 3 |   |   |   |   |   |   |   |
| 4 |   |   |   |   |   |   |   |
| 5 |   |   |   |   |   |   |   |
| 6 |   |   |   |   |   |   |   |
| 7 |   |   |   |   |   |   |   |
| 8 |   |   |   |   |   |   |   |

| B2 | E4 | E3 | ■ |   | B6 | B1 | E7 | F8 | B4 | ■ |
|----|----|----|---|---|----|----|----|----|----|---|
| T  |    |    | ■ |   |    |    |    |    |    | ■ |
| A7 | A3 | B8 | D2 | E8 | E5 | G2 | F1 | ■ |
|    |    |    |    |    |    |    |    | ■ |
| C4 | A6 | ■  | E2 | F5 | G1 | C7 | G3 |
|    |    | ■  |    |    |    |    |    |

# HOAX?

The arrival of anonymous letters received at Poirot's London address raised the possibility of a hoax.

**Here is a mystery message. Is this also a hoax?**

The letters **A**, **B** and **C** in the message have all been replaced by the letter X. The other letters of the alphabet are in their correct places.

**Can you unravel the mystery and discover the message?**

X XXRD XRRIVED IN THE

LXST POST.

ON XXLXNXE, THE XOXXH

XRXSH XXN BE XXLLED XN

XXXIDENT XS XLXIMED.

# WHERE AM I?

Where will the sender of the below puzzle strike next?  Use the clues in the rhymes to name the place.

My first is in murder,

And also in crime.

My second is in find,

And also in time.

My third is in suspect,

And also in plan.

My fourth is in open,

But isn't in began.

My fifth is in lane,

But isn't in place.

Where will I strike next?

At a ground that hosts a race!

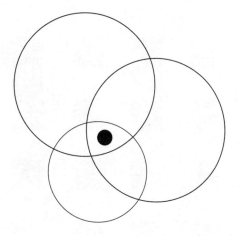

# ALPHABET CROSSWORD

There are twenty-six letters of the alphabet. There are twenty-six clues. Each answer begins with a different letter of the alphabet.

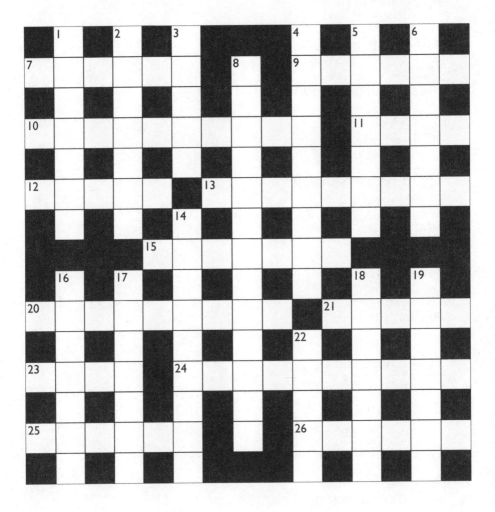

Below is the starter letter and the number of letters in each answer. It's up to you to work out where to put the answers in the grid . . .

A   Attack violently (7)

B   Devon resort near the home of the Carmichaels (7)

C   A police officer (9)

D   The first name of Betty Barnard's boyfriend (6)

E   Modifies and checks a document (5)

F   Illumination from coal or wood burning in a hearth (9)

G   Rise to a standing position (3.2)

H   Well, in good physical condition (7)

I   Bad feeling (3.4)

J   Prison (4)

K   Murdered (6)

L   Merciful, not severe with regard to a punishment (7)

M   There are sixty in an hour (7)

N   Soft fruits, similar to peaches (10)

O   Being too clever for an opponent and showing greater ingenuity (10)

P   Calm in difficult circumstances (13)

Q   Making little or no noise (7)

R   Respond, perhaps to a letter (5)

S   Proposed a hypothesis or a plan of action (9)

T   Colossal, and the name of an ocean liner which sank in the North Atlantic in 1912 (7)

U   Disturbance or agitation (6)

V   Person with exceptional foresight (9)

W   Bereaved husband, such a Franz Aschel, whose wife was the first ABC victim (7)

X   December festive season (4)

Y   Measurements of three feet (5)

Z   Plucked, stringed musical instrument (6)

# LINKS

Can you work out what links most of these messages together?
I say 'most' as there is one message which doesn't have that link.
Can you work out why?

1. Rory our poetry tutor wrote to you.

2. Our priority? Your quiet trip to Truro!

3. We try out our tour route.

4. You two! Quit our territory!

5. We played with our pet puppy.

Dear Aunt Mary,

Having at first embraced my predicament, I am finding the role a rather lonely affair without Mrs Ashmore's promised guidance during my first week here at Greenway.

I have reordered the shelves which, on closer inspection, were in a rather odd state. Mrs Ashmore must have decided to alphabetise the books the library holds - which include some beautifully crafted first editions - and had started this process, but seemingly vanished before she could finish.

Piled in random corners throughout the room were stacks of books, with one pile tottering so precariously high I could not let it go on. Marching over, I started pulling titles from the top as gently as I could, but of course only managed to make the entire column unstable. A first edition copy of *The ABC Murders* fell to the floor with a thud, opening around halfway through to reveal a new bundle.

I quickly scooped up the puzzles and, hearing footsteps, turned towards the door, but it was only the cook asking if I was wanting any tea. He asked me how I was settling in and remarked how 'Agnes' would

never have let the library get into such a
state. Rather than prickle at his incorrect
and slightly harsh words, I realised Mrs
<u>A</u>gnes <u>A</u>shmore would have been the perfect
victim for the ABC killer.

I hope all is well with you, dear aunt,
and I await your help.

Your nephew,

Charles

# DOUBLE DEAL

Solve the clues and write your answers in the grid. As befits an ABC puzzle, there is an alphabetical link. There is just one letter of the alphabet which does not appear in any of the answers. What is it?

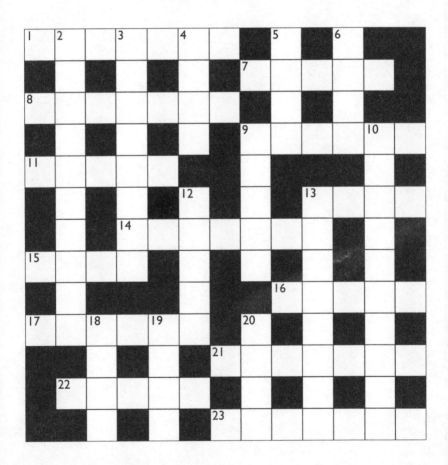

ACROSS

1 Laid the blame on (7)

7 The other Miss Barnard (5)

8 Moving vehicles (7)

9 Entices (6)

11 Aviator (5)

13 Notoriety (4)

14 Line round the centre of the Earth (7)

15 Daybreak (4)

16 Spouse's relation (2,3)

17 Wall recess (6)

21 Four-stringed guitar (7)

22 First name of the first victim (5)

23 From Madrid! (7)

DOWN

2 First name of the Churston victim (10)

3 Thawed (8)

4 Way out (4)

5 Outdoor function (4)

6 Chief investigating officer of the ABC murders (4)

9 Veracity (5)

10 Lists of arrivals and departures by train (10)

12 Book of essential information (5)

13 The younger Clarke brother (8)

18 Peace, tranquillity (4)

19 Immoral conduct (4)

20 Jump lightly over a rope (4)

# CHAPTER 6

# Dead Man's Folly

AT THE FÊTE

HOOPLA

TRUE FOLLY

WATER-WAYS

YHA

JUST THE OPPOSITE

WORD WALL

RAFFLE WINNERS

GARDENS AND GROUNDS

JIGSAW PIECES

# AT THE FÊTE

Sir George and Lady Stubbs have opened the grounds of their home for a summer fête. In the word search square below, you will find some of the attractions on offer. The words appear in straight lines across, backwards, up, down and diagonally. There is one word in the list which appears three times and there is one word that doesn't appear at all. **Will you be able to work it out?**

```
C F T N U H N O I S S I M D A
O O S E T A G Y S E B S R J E
N L C I N N X E S O E E A Z S
T L P O I T R O A L L M I D J
E Y X G N D R T B L S R W P N
S A D X Y U H A E L P O A A O
T U L C A O T T N U R I S T I
J L N D U V E S G C D S S H T
W A P S Q N H C H K E B L S I
F W E E U Q R A M Y L L O F T
U N P T T A U K S D L A P V E
L S R E F U J E M I G L E T P
M O A F N P A S U P R Y O L M
F S L L A T S O T E N T S F O
V E G E T A B L E S E E R T C
```

| | |
|---|---|
| ADMISSION | MARQUEE |
| BOATHOUSE | NASSE |
| CAKES | PAID |
| COCONUT SHY | PATHS |
| COMPETITION | PRIZE |
| CONTEST | QUAY |
| CROWDS | QUEUE |
| ENTRANCE | RAFFLE |
| FANCY DRESS | ROSES |
| FOLLY | SEAT |
| FORTUNE TELLER | SKITTLES |
| GATES | SLOPE |
| HUNT | STALLS |
| JAMS | TEAS |
| JUDGING | TENTS |
| LAWNS | TREES |
| LUCKY DIP | VEGETABLES |

# HOOPLA

You will definitely have to jump through hoops with this puzzle. Two hoops from the hoopla stall at the fête have found their way here. Solve the clues and work out which hoop the answers belong to. The last two letters of one answer are the first two of the next, so words overlap, and all answers have FIVE letters.

I doubt you will be able to complete this without help, so: the first answer of **Hoop A** is **STAGE** and the first answer of **Hoop B** is **SERVE**.

1.  Arrange a performance such as a Murder Hunt
    * Act as a waiter or waitress in the tea tent
2.  Style of writing, such as Mrs Oliver's crime novels
    * Wild plant of the pea family
3.  The ringing of a grandfather clock
    * Go over previously known information
4.  Substance the blade of a knife is made from
    * Mrs Oliver's favourite fruit
5.  Lawful
    * Change, such as with someone's appearance
6.  Wear away, destroy gradually
    * A false or assumed name
7.  A score of forty all in tennis
    * Garden plant with daisy-like flowers
8.  A variety of heather
    * Evergreen tree found in the grounds of large estates
9.  Capture a culprit
    * Where the action takes place
10. A large box for storing
    * The house in *Dead Man's Folly*

**HOOP A**

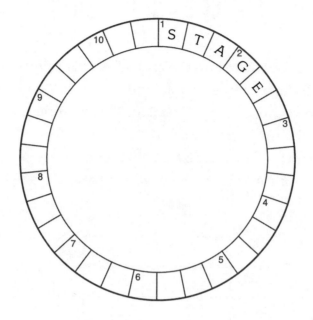

**HOOP B**

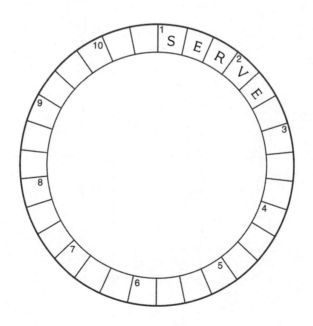

# TRUE FOLLY

Fit the words opposite into the grid. All words have SEVEN letters and have links with the people and places in *Dead Man's Folly*. Twelve words need to be slotted in. There is one letter to start. Words read either across or down.

As with the victims at Nasse House, there is a stroke of bad luck for a thirteenth word, which has no place in the grid. What is it?

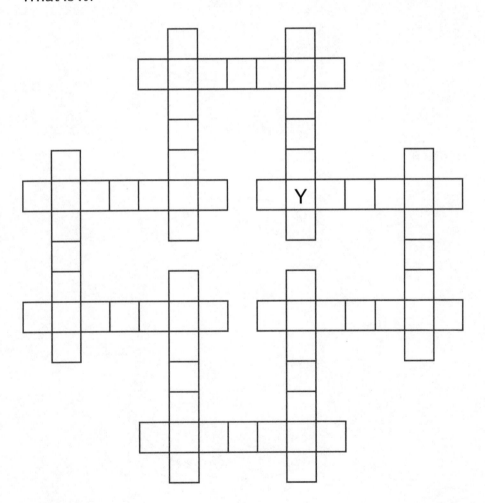

ARIADNE

CHARITY

FICTION

FOLLIAT

HOSTELS

ITALIAN

KILLING

MANSION

MARILYN

MERDELL

MURDERS

MYSTERY

WEALTHY

# WATER-WAYS

Two words of equal length are combined into a single line of letters. The letters of individual words remain in sequence. All words link to locations with water. Good luck.

1. F L O A R K D E

2. L M E O R C E H

3. B C R A O N A O K L

4. C O C E R E A E N K

5. F R I E R A T H C H

6. M R A R I S V E H R

7. L S T A R G E O A O N M

8. C E H S A N T N U A E R Y L

# YHA

The backpackers at the Youth Hostel adjoining Nasse House seem to be a constant source of annoyance to Sir George and the other residents. Their likes and dislikes were not always the same. Here are the views of some of the backpackers who were staying at the hostel run by the YHA.

---

## Backpacker 1

I always wear a HAT, never a BERET. When I am sitting on the grass, I always sit on a MAT, not a RUG. I prefer to be OUT rather than IN and get a TAXI rather than a BUS.

---

## Backpacker 2

I enjoy walking by the MOUTH of the river rather than UPSTREAM. I like it when it's HOT rather than COLD. I prefer to HUM a tune rather than SING.

---

## Backpacker 3

I love dogs, especially the TOY group. I like the IVY which climbs up house walls, rather than the WISTERIA. I am inquisitive and always want to know WHY and HOW things happen.

There IS a reason why these things are liked or disliked. It's a question of how you look at things. Poirot himself reflects in *Dead Man's Folly* that 'If one knew what to look for, it would be so easy.'

**What is the link?**

# JUST THE OPPOSITE

Sometimes, the person you expect to have committed a crime proves to be just the opposite. In this crossword, the principle is the same. The solution is the opposite of the clue.

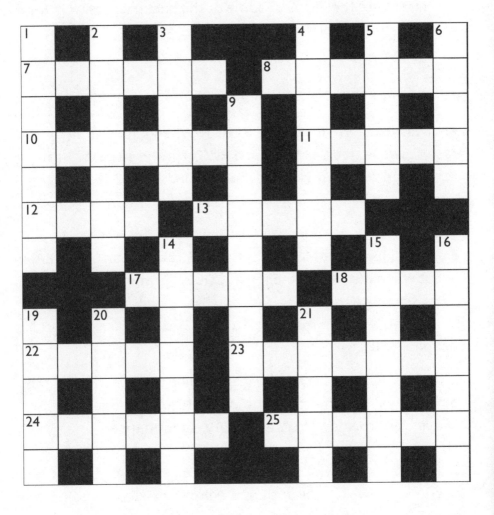

## ACROSS

7 Entered (6)
8 Disciple (6)
10 Sturdy (7)
11 Small (5)
12 Neglect (4)
13 Mistaken (5)
17 Extrovert (5)
18 Clothed (4)
22 Sufficient (5)
23 Bury (7)
24 Novice (6)
25 Awake (6)

## DOWN

1 Flawed (7)
2 Ordinary (7)
3 Safety (5)
4 Impoverished (7)
5 Loathe (5)
6 Chaos (5)
9 Inedible (9)
14 Cooperation (7)
15 Ambled (7)
16 Certainly (7)
19 Undulating (5)
20 Begins (5)
21 Relaxed (5)

# WORD WALL

Below is a panel of words with FIVE columns going down and FOUR rows going across. The instructions will tell you which words to take away from the wall. When you have completed this task, you will be left with just THREE words describing a famous character.

|   | A | B | C | D | E |
|---|---|---|---|---|---|
| 1 | HASTINGS | EGG | MANOR | BLONDE | LEMON |
| 2 | AUBURN | ROMAN | APPLES | SHAPED | WHEEL |
| 3 | TRAFALGAR | WAIT | PLATE | FERRY | OAR |
| 4 | FÊTE | NORMA | GREY | HELM | HEAD |

Take away all the words which are anagrams of each other.
Take away the names of any hair colours.
Take away any names with a boating link in columns D and E.
Take away any words that rhyme with a word meaning destiny.
Take away any names who are associated with helping Poirot in row 1.
Take away Mrs Oliver's favourite fruit.
Take away a word with a square link which is Poirot's London telephone exchange.

**Which words remain?**

# RAFFLE WINNERS

As well as the murder mystery, one of the biggest attractions at the fête held in the grounds of Nasse House is the magnificent raffle. Fun and fundraising combine as everyone who attends and buys a ticket has a chance to land a prize.

The first prize was a pig. Second prize was a fabulous hamper of fruit, third was a rose bush, fourth was a sponge cake and the fifth prize was a doll.

In number order, the five winning tickets were 111, 183, 222, 289 and 308.

**From the clues, can you match the prizes with the raffle tickets and the names of the winners?**

## CLUES

1. The prize for raffle ticket 183 had been handed out directly before Julie Brewer, a local farmer's wife, claimed her prize. She had a raffle ticket with a number showing the same digit three times.
2. Matt Hands, the local odd job man, did not win the fifth prize. He was hoping to win the rose bush, but that had already been claimed by a ticket that contained no odd digits.
3. Both the verger and Adam Ploughman, a gardener, were disappointed when Miss Joy Pollitt claimed the pig.
4. There was only the doll to hand out after the cake was claimed by the owner of ticket 289.
5. The third prize went to the third highest number of the winning tickets. The verger had the highest number of all the winners.
6. The winner of the fruit had the ticket with the lowest number.

# GARDENS AND GROUNDS

The gardens and grounds at Nasse House were planned and planted with great care. The diagram shows the land divided into individual square areas. The numbers indicate how many flowering bushes are next to that area.

As part of the scheme, no bush can be horizontally, vertically or diagonally next to another bush. No bushes appear in any of the numbered areas. Note well, that the letters **N** and **B** appear on the plan. **B** stands for **BUSH** and **N** stands for **NO**, meaning no bushes can go in that area.

**From this information can you work out where all the bushes need to be planted?**

| | | | | | | | | |
|---|---|---|---|---|---|---|---|---|
| 1 | 2 | N | 1 | | | 2 | | 1 |
| | N | B | N | | | | | |
| | N | N | N | | | | | |
| | 2 | | | | 4 | | | 2 |
| | | | | | | | 2 | |
| | | | | | | | | |
| 1 | | | 3 | | | | | 1 |
| | | | | 1 | 3 | | | |
| | 1 | | | | 1 | | 2 | |

# JIGSAW PIECES

Poirot is doing a jigsaw in his London home. In this puzzle, a
9 x 9 crossword has been broken up into nine jigsaw pieces. The
first three letters going down in the top left-hand corner of the
completed puzzle are **WRO**.

**Can you put the remaining pieces back together and complete
the jigsaw?**

| W | | | | | | | | |
|---|---|---|---|---|---|---|---|---|
| R | | | | | | | | |
| O | | | | | | | | |
| | | | | | | | | |
| | | | | | | | | |
| | | | | | | | | |
| | | | | | | | | |
| | | | | | | | | |
| | | | | | | | | |

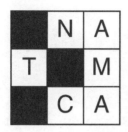

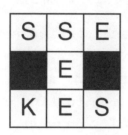

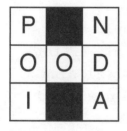

Dear Aunt Mary,

As much as I hesitate at accusing a fellow librarian of negligence, I have come to the surprising conclusion that Mrs Ashmore was not all she said she was. The library is in dire need of a complete rehaul and has even begun to take on a peculiar smell.

Trying to locate any particular book for members of the house is near impossible. I have a missing librarian, and a missing book, too. I cannot seem to find one single copy of *Dead Man's Folly* anywhere I look. There is a beautiful painting of Nasse House hanging on the library wall, however, and knowing of Mrs Ashmore's propensity for the dramatic, I thought there could be a secret nook behind it. Finding only a flat wall, I became despondent until realising the painting itself was hiding a new bundle stapled to the back of the canvas.

I do fear, dear aunt, I may be on my own Murder Hunt before long.

Please do write back, I am beginning to worry.

Your nephew,

Charles

# MOVING ON

---

Are these numbered statements meaningless?
Are they another folly, a construction which
serves no real purpose? Who can say, but it
is time to move on.

---

What is the missing word at the end of 7?

---

1. No clue.

2. No clue.

3. No clue.

4. It was a banjo hidden in the ferns.

5. He drank the fizz while on one knee.

6. On the silver chain hung a gold ingot.

7. Throughout the entire hotel,

   a pattern of _____.

# CHAPTER 7

# Death on the Nile

PUZZLING PYRAMID

WHO SAID THAT?

HIEROGLYPHICS

BURIAL CHAMBERS

TRIPLICATIONS

INTERLOCKED

BACK TO FRONT

MISUNDERSTOOD

DISEMBARKING

THE SUM OF A PYRAMID

# PUZZLING PYRAMID

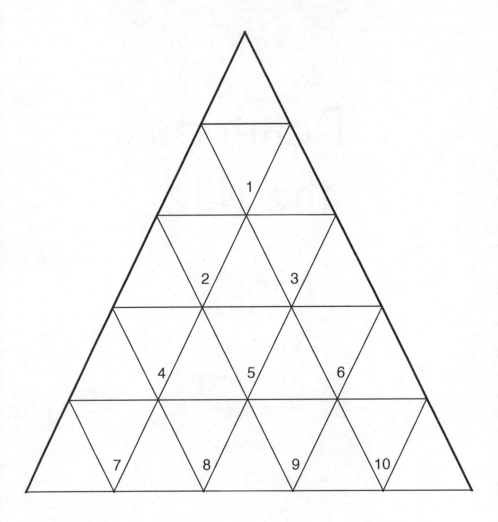

Each answer to the clues below contains FOUR letters. The first letter goes in a numbered triangle, the second letter directly above it, the third letter to the right and the fourth to the left.

**Can you complete the pyramid?**

1. First name of Dr Bessner, the Austrian doctor and psychologist

2. A plot or strategy, as hatched by Simon and Jacqueline

3. A region, or tract of land

4. Had information

5. This word describes finds and artefacts which are uncommon

6. Cherished or expensive

7. If things go this way, then chaos ensues

8. A Lord, such as Lord Windlesham who was cast aside by Linnet in favour of Simon

9. At liberty

10. Not genuine, as was the case with Mrs Doyle's substituted 'pearls'

# WHO SAID THAT?

Answer the questions and slot them into their correct places in the below grid. All answers have SEVEN letters. When this grid is complete, read the first column reading down to reveal the name of 'who said that'.

Take the letters in the keycoded squares and write them in the grid opposite. When complete, the words will reveal a quotation by a character from *Death on the Nile*.

Rearrange the letters in the shaded squares to discover where those words were spoken on the trip to the Nile.

|    | A | B | C | D | E | F | G |
|----|---|---|---|---|---|---|---|
| 1  |   |   |   |   |   |   |   |
| 2  |   |   |   |   |   |   |   |
| 3  |   |   |   |   |   |   |   |
| 4  |   |   |   |   |   |   |   |
| 5  |   |   |   |   |   |   |   |
| 6  |   |   |   |   |   |   |   |
| 7  |   |   |   |   |   |   |   |
| 8  |   |   |   |   |   |   |   |
| 9  |   |   |   |   |   |   |   |
| 10 |   |   |   |   |   |   |   |

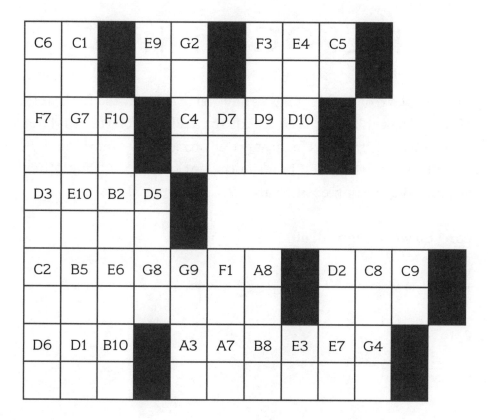

1. Mrs Allerton and Mrs Otterbourne, for example
2. Talks at length about nothing in particular
3. Great wealth, as possessed by Linnet Ridgeway
4. Travel extensively to discover new things
5. Alarmed or disconcerted as to how events are unfolding
6. Sparkle or flash brilliantly like precious gems
7. Dig up, as an archaeologist might do
8. A person at a school or college, like Linnet or Jacqueline when they were in Paris
9. Not indoors
10. Not one or the other

# HIEROGLYPHICS

Hieroglyphs from Ancient Egypt have been substituted for letters of the alphabet. Each shape stands for a different letter, and the code does not change. The first group stands for something that was very important to Linnet and went missing. All the other groups give the names of related valuable items.

**Can you work them all out?**

1.

2.

3.

4.

5.

# BURIAL CHAMBERS

Here is a maze of underground tunnels that house burial chambers of the pharaohs of Ancient Egypt. Find a route to visit the three tombs in the order 1, 2 and then 3. You must find an alternative route back to the entrance.

To avoid falling foul of a centuries-old curse, you must not use the same path or path junction twice. Or I will find you . . .

# TRIPLICATIONS

In each of the sentences below, there is ONE word which is an anagram three different ways. The same letters appear in three different combinations to make three different words. Can you figure them out? I've included an example for you, just to make sure you can do it — I don't trust your smarts.

1.  Neil had to draw the line as to how many temples they had time to visit on their Nile cruise.

2.  Lawyer _ _ _ _ _ _ Pennington allowed his mind to _ _ _ _ _ _ as he looked out of the window. He had been _ _ _ _ _ _ that disaster might lie ahead.

3.  'Je _ _ _ _ _ français, comme M. Poirot,' said Jacqueline. She was gazing at the beautiful _ _ _ _ _ necklace. The colour of each exquisite sphere was _ _ _ _ _ than she remembered.

4.  Miss Ridgeway was determined to improve the land and _ _ _ _ _ _ which surrounded the huge house. Changes _ _ _ _ _ _ from building a swimming pool to evicting existing tenants.  There was a _ _ _ _ _ _ that she would become very unpopular.

**5.** They had all heard _ _ _ _ _ of how there were those on board who wished to _ _ _ _ _ what they could from the rich passengers. The _ _ _ _ _ they could do was take advice from the famous detective.

**6.** A _ _ _ _ _ such as Devon had many families with _ _ _ _ _ to a small fortune. In a dramatic incident, someone who would not inherit _ _ _ _ _ an assassin to make sure he receives an inheritance.

**7.** The boat was powered by _ _ _ _ _. _ _ _ _ _ _ of experienced cabin crew and ship _ _ _ _ _, such as engineers, made sure that the journey was as enjoyable as possible.

# INTERLOCKED

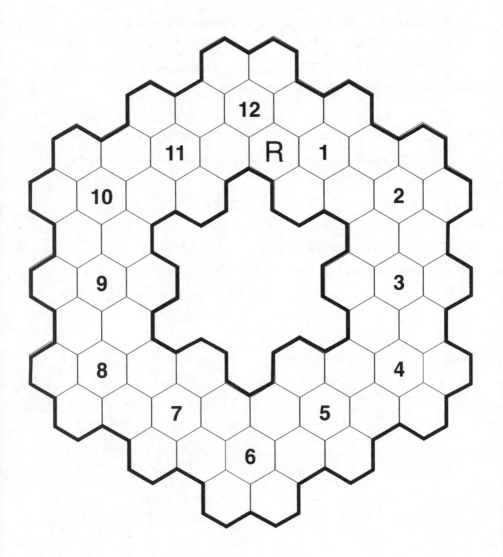

Solve the clues and place them in the grid reading in a CLOCKWISE direction, so that they interlock with each other. All answers have SIX letters (the second letter of answer 1 is R). It is up to you to solve the remaining clues and work out where each answer begins, if you dare try.

## CLUES

1.  Move around from place to place, go on a journey

2.  Deadly

3.  French port on the English Channel, the nearest to England

4.  Coins used in France in the 1930s

5.  Sea which is a bay of the Mediterranean between Asia and Europe

6.  Country, capital Athens

7.  Climb

8.  Form of address to a married lady, a term frequently used by Poirot

9.  Respect, held in high worth

10. Another word for a language

11. Reacts to something amusing, a common reaction from Jacqueline

12. Precious gems produced by oysters, Linnet's favourite necklace

# BACK TO FRONT

Poirot is taking a holiday aboard the Nile steamer Karnak, a name in which its first two letters reflect the last two.

The answers to the clues here follow this very same pattern, where letters one and two are the other way round in the penultimate and final letters.

## CLUES

1. A comfortable chair with a leaning position for relaxing on deck

   _____

2. A collection of matching china used at a light afternoon meal

   _____

3. Describes a desirable or suitable partner in marriage, such as Linnet Ridgeway

   _____

4. A dainty morsel of food, or a piece of gossip!

   _____

**5.** Thoroughfares in the towns, such as where Karnak docked

_____

**6.** No longer alive

_____

**7.** An amount over and above what is needed

_____

**8.** A capricious or absurd idea

_____

**9.** To wholeheartedly adopt a cause

_____

**10.** Develop gradually, such as with a plan or theory

_____

# MISUNDERSTOOD

Karnak passenger Miss Van Schuyler is rather hard of hearing and cannot be relied upon to hear things accurately. In each clue one word has been deliberately misspelt and, therefore, makes no sense. Work out which word is 'misunderstood' and put the correct answer in the grid.

## ACROSS

1 It is a lateral translation from the original (7)

7 It is important to use your drain cells during an investigation (5)

8 Fortunately a crisis was alerted (7)

9 They threw the banker overboard so that the ship was secure (6)

11 Attic is a savoury meat jelly filled with game or eggs (5)

13 A murderer was often sentenced to hand (4)

14 It was a ghostly sight when the crime was discovered (7)

15 At the village inn they kept beer in wooden legs (4)

16 It was udder chaos in the village when the cows escaped (5)

17 Bread is part of a stable diet in most countries (6)

21 Parrots are a traditional accompaniment to British roast beef (7)

22 The lawyer lines the letter at the bottom of the page (5)

23 Everything was finished other than a few minor derails (7)

## DOWN

2 Her divestment was not producing enough interest (10)

3 Their crime was to make a living from dubious earrings (8)

4 Omen is the last word of a prayer (4)

5 His statement gave rise to a broad Gran (4)

6 It is my greatest fish that this event takes place (4)

9 We are hoping the storm will await and then we can go outside (5)

10 Poirot possessed a monumental fly whisk with a sham amber handle (10)

12 The captain was wearing his barge of office (5)

13 When the murder was discovered there was mass wisteria on board (8)

18 The lord was an arid supporter of village events (4)

19 It had been a lung journey down the river (4)

20 Tea was served, with scones, cream and a delicious slice of hake (4)

# DISEMBARKING

On its journey down the River Nile, the steamer Karnak would occasionally pull to shore and moor for a short break. On one such stop, five passengers disembarked. They were, in alphabetical order: **Tim Allerton**, **Jacqueline de Bellefort**, **Simon Doyle**, **Salome Otterbourne** and **Andrew Pennington**.

Each of the individuals left the steamer on their own and returned on their own.

On disembarking, each lady had a gentleman leave the steamer directly before her, and had a gentleman leave the steamer directly after her.

None of the gentlemen either disembarked or embarked in the same position as their name when read in alphabetical order.

Jacqueline de Bellefort disembarked directly after Simon Doyle.

When returning to the steamer the ladies followed each other but neither was first. The three gentlemen followed each other.

No one had the same disembarking and embarking position.

**Who was first to go back on board?**

# THE SUM OF A PYRAMID

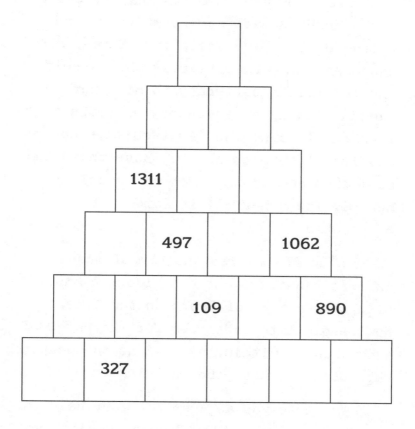

Can you write a number on every stone in this pyramid, so that every number will be the total of the numbers on the two stones directly below it?

When the pyramid is complete, add up the numbers that appear in each row. There is one digit from 0 to 9 that does not appear in the totals. **What is it?**

Dear Aunt Mary,

A worrisome few days indeed have just passed.

A visit from a solicitor has revealed Mrs Ashmore's vast debts, which she has tried to hide for some years. I fear she has been using the disarray she herself invited into the library to hide her real agenda. Taking an inventory of books this morning, I found two first-edition copies missing. I surmise she may have tried to sell them and, due to her unscrupulous scheme, found herself in some sort of trouble.

I also discovered another of Mrs Ashmore's quirks. She has hidden a small pistol in a copy of *Death on the Nile*, hollowed out to make room for the pages of a new bundle within, as well as the weapon. Why would she need such a thing?

I write to you as ever for your help in completing the most difficult puzzle I've encountered so far. My usual capacities for finding solutions have been dulled by the malodorous smell of the library. I cannot find its source, but I am determined to find the handyman instead and utilise his tools in prising apart the room.

Whilst I wait for him, I am applying
myself to a history of Greenway I found,
to learn any information that may be helpful
in my current circumstances.

I will find the source of this mystery.

Your nephew,

Charles

# VOWEL PLAY

Crack the cryptic crossword with vowel play at work.

ACROSS

7 Astute assessment of sculptured work of art (6)

9 Infallible guide or a clear appearance (6)

10 Ensure no division in restored decoration (10)

11 Alter diet for sea change (4)

12 Keen to agree differently (5)

13 Lamenting restructured bringing into line (9)

15 Fixed and focused (7)

20 It was revealed that the part I choked on was related to the thistle (9)

21 Soil dug up at the centre (5)

23 Avoid young lady (4)

24 The short duration of sliced nectarines (10)

25 Signed over prototype (6)

26 Apprehend the rarest destroyer (6)

DOWN

1 Box seat dating from the empire (7)

2 Tales from various floors, we hear (7)

3 Ancient piece of sorrel I collected and exposed (5)

4 One from overseas in front of confused royal rule (9)

5 Migrate over syncopated music (7)

6 Specifically indulge avoidance (7)

8 Lack real pence to afford valuable choker (5,8)

14 Resist accompanying spectator seats (9)

16 Curse is cast on Egyptian river trips (7)

17 Sink oil to provide waterproof garment (7)

18 Shooting stars from a remote point (7)

19 Exact recooked recipes (7)

22 Ancient Egyptian city as wanderer discovered (5)

# CHAPTER 8

# The Body in the Library

MASK-ERADE

BROUGHT TO BOOK

ANYONE FOR TENNIS?

THE MAJESTIC HOTEL

RED HERRINGS

CARDS ON THE TABLE

TAKE YOUR PARTNERS

ROUTE MAP

LAST WILL AND TESTAMENT

MISS MARPLE'S WORDS

# MASK-ERADE

In this puzzle, words are linked to the lives of the glamorous dancers at the Majestic Hotel, and slot into the grid across and down. There is only one solution that will use all the words . . . Try if you dare.

## 3 LETTERS
ADD
BAG
EYE
RED
TOE

## 4 LETTERS
COMB
DYED
EVEN
FACE
JARS
KOHL
LIPS
NECK
OILS
SNIP

## 5 LETTERS
APPLY
BASIN
BLUSH
BRUSH
ELBOW
HENNA
RINSE
ROUGE
SCENT
TONIC
TOUCH

## 6 LETTERS
LASHES
MIRROR
PALEST
SHAPES

## 7 LETTERS
BOUQUET
DROPLET
PERFUME

## 8 LETTERS
AROMATIC
COMPACTS
COSMETIC
HAIRCLIP
MANICURE

## 9 LETTERS
FRAGRANCE
HAND CREAM
LIPSTICKS

## 10 LETTERS
ASTRINGENT

## 11 LETTERS
LOOSE POWDER
NAIL VARNISH

## 12 LETTERS
TALCUM POWDER

## 14 LETTERS
CLEANSING CREAM
VANISHING CREAM

# BROUGHT TO BOOK

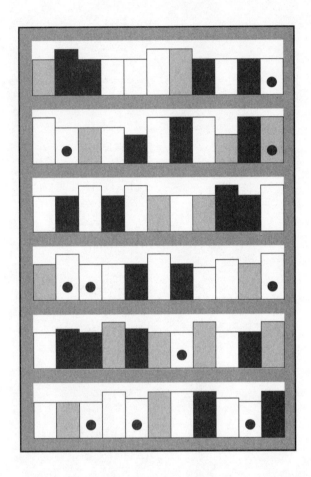

Miss Marple has lent a book to Dolly Bantry, which has ended up on the shelves of the library in Gossington Hall. **Can you locate the book from the clues to return the book back to Miss Marple?**

The book is on a row where three tall books only just fit the shelf height.
The book does not have a black circle on the spine.
The book is between a white book and a grey book.
The book is directly below a black book.

# ANYONE FOR TENNIS?

The annual tennis tournament at the Majestic Hotel is a splendid affair. It is a chance for the fashionable ladies of the area to show that they have immaculate taste.

One hundred and twenty ladies attended the event.

90 per cent of the ladies wore hats.

Three quarters of the ladies sported brightly coloured floral dresses.

Precisely 112 ladies wore a necklace, which was twice the number of ladies who carried a parasol.

**What is the smallest possible number of ladies to wear a hat, a floral dress, a necklace and carry a parasol?**

# THE MAJESTIC HOTEL

Words linked to the Majestic Hotel in the coastal resort of Danemouth can be found below in the letter grid. Words are in straight lines but can go across, down, forwards, backwards and on any of the diagonals!

One word is present three times and one word in the list is not in the grid . . . Adopt Miss Marple's powers of observation to discover what these are.

```
B Q U R E N T R A P E C N A D
R A G U E S T E N N I S E S B
E T L N J O N C A S E S K A A
A X R L S E T I U S E N S E T
K B E D R O O M A R I V E T H
F O N N B O R C O R R I D O R
A O N A M R O O D E R S L V O
S K I P E C L M C S Y I K A O
T E D C K F E E T T R T V C M
U D N T E N W A C A S E S A F
N A A C U A B L O U N G E T L
D I N S I L U S E R V I C E O
L A W T E N P B N A I X A T O
D R E S C O U C H N M V O G R
O R C H E S T R A T E K E Y S
```

ARRIVAL

BALLROOM

BATHROOM

BEDROOM

BOOKED

BREAKFAST

CASES

COCKTAIL

CORRIDOR

COUCH

COURTYARD

DANCE FLOOR

DANCE PARTNER

DANCER

DESK

DINNER

DOORMAN

DRINKS

FLOORS

GUEST

KEYS

LEAVE

LOUNGE

LUNCH

MEALS

MENUS

MUSIC

ORCHESTRA

RESTAURANT

SERVICE

SUITE

TABLES

TAXI

TEAS

TENNIS

VACATE

VISIT

WAITER

# RED HERRINGS

To double cross means to deceive. In this puzzle, I will go one step further and present a triple cross!

Fit the correct words into the grid. There are three words to choose from. There is only one way to slot them into the grid so that they all fit. You have a one-word start: the answer to **12 across** is **BOOK**.

**Can you fish out the red herrings?**

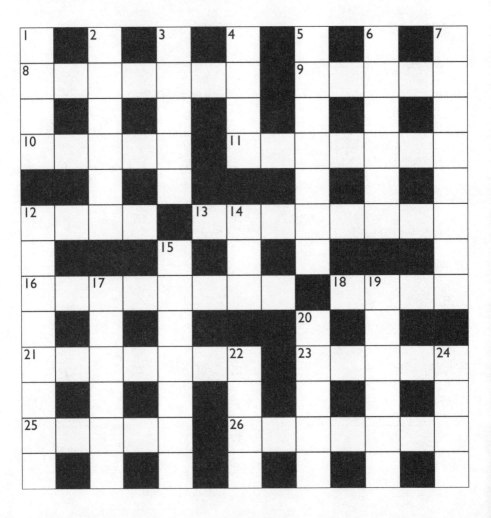

## ACROSS

8 Attract * Collude * Cottage
9 Choir * Flood * Floor
10 Elder * Ended * Enter
11 Diagram * Interim * Quarrel
12 Bank * Book * Cook
13 Charming * Children * Explored
16 Misleads * Suspects * Suspends
18 Bell * Hall * Hill
21 Bashful * Bluffed * Scuffle
23 Tonic * Topaz * Topic
25 Décor * Diner * Lunch
26 Avarice * Unaware * Useless

## DOWN

1 Acre * Ices * Scan
2 Strand * Strong * Studio
3 Marry * Maxim * Merry
4 Owed * Read * Road
5 Affable * Capable * Offence
6 Horror * Mirror * Porter
7 Comments * Criminal * Presents
12 Busybody * Bystander * Disobeys
14 Hat * Hoe * How
15 Confirm * Perform * Perjury
17 Saying * Square * Squint
19 Abroad * Appear * Aspect
20 Appal * Speak * Steal
22 Drug * Plug * Snug
24 Beef * Chef * Feed

# CARDS ON THE TABLE

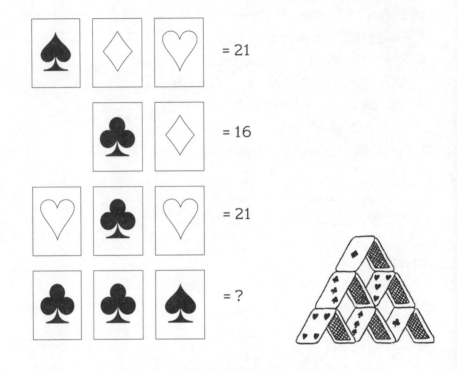

♠ ◇ ♡ = 21

♣ ◇ = 16

♡ ♣ ♡ = 21

♣ ♣ ♠ = ?

Bridge was one of the favourite pastimes of many of the guests at the Majestic Hotel.

Under Josie's watchful eye, a group have invented a new game. Each ace is given a numerical value.

The value cannot be higher than nine. No two different suits can have the same number. The values of the cards in a row are added together. The players have to work out the values of the cards.

**Fancy a game? Try your hand and work out the total value of the bottom row of cards.**

# TAKE YOUR PARTNERS

Ruby Keene was part of the dance team at the Majestic Hotel. Here, the names of dances are hidden in sentences. Find them by joining words or parts of words together — but hurry, the orchestra is about to play. . .

**CLUES**

1. In the Highlands, tartan goes swinging from side to side as the dancers in their kilts begin.

2. Are you sure elite dancers will take part in the competition?

3. At the church social event the new deacon gave out the prizes.

4. Beating a drum bangs out a rhythm which everyone can follow.

5. During the interval several people took the opportunity of getting some fresh air.

6. Someone looking very suave let all the dancers on to the ballroom floor.

# ROUTE MAP

A body is discovered in a quarry two miles from Danemouth. Which route might the murderer and victim have taken between the two locations? There would be very few cars driving through the twisted narrow country roads early in the morning. Police enquiries did reveal that seven separate households noted that a single car had gone past their property. No one could recall in which direction the vehicle was heading.

The murderer and unfortunate victim must have gone by the seven properties marked with an X. The householders were sure there were no other vehicles on the road, so they could not have gone down the same road twice.

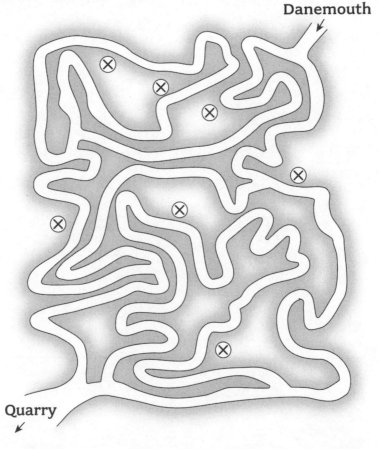

# LAST WILL AND TESTAMENT

Conway Jefferson went along with Miss Marple's plan to suggest he was going to alter his will so that there would be a change of beneficiary to his great wealth.

The writer of the below message has had the foresight to conceal the terms of his last will and testament too, in a very secret way.

**Do you have the same foresight? Can you work out who will inherit?**

> *I hope that all my friends after*
> *my death will acquire fortune.*
> *Terms of my will mean*
> *everyone can benefit.*
> *My very favourite charities*
> *deserve this. So, close as we are*
> *to when you miss me,*
> *I send you best and most*
> *heartfelt wishes.*

# MISS MARPLE'S WORDS

Solve the clues below and write the answers to read across in their correct places in the larger grid. All answers have NINE letters.

When this grid is complete, take the letters in the keycoded squares and write them in the smaller grid. When the smaller grid is complete, the words will reveal a quotation by Miss Marple from *The Body in the Library*. The quotation begins, 'A well-bred girl would never turn up . . .'

In addition, rearrange the letters in the centre shaded column reading down (column E) to spell out the name of another major character in the book.

## CLUES

1. A piece of dining room furniture which holds china, cutlery etc.

2. A false or assumed name

3. Describes a chatterbox or a village gossip

4. A dancer like Ruby, or an actor, singer or musician

5. The home of the cinema industry in the USA

6. Person who records the action on film

7. Exciting

8. Intolerant, not able to wait for something or someone

9. Information, a range of facts, vital in solving a case

10. Two weeks

11. The holiday following a wedding

|   | A | B | C | D | E | F | G | H | I |
|---|---|---|---|---|---|---|---|---|---|
| 1 |   |   |   |   |   |   |   |   |   |
| 2 |   |   |   |   |   |   |   |   |   |
| 3 |   |   |   |   |   |   |   |   |   |
| 4 |   |   |   |   |   |   |   |   |   |
| 5 |   |   |   |   |   |   |   |   |   |
| 6 |   |   |   |   |   |   |   |   |   |
| 7 |   |   |   |   |   |   |   |   |   |
| 8 |   |   |   |   |   |   |   |   |   |
| 9 |   |   |   |   |   |   |   |   |   |
| 10 |   |   |   |   |   |   |   |   |   |
| 11 |   |   |   |   |   |   |   |   |   |

| G1 | F3 | ■ | F6 | ■ | C8 | C9 | F10 | C11 | A7 | ■ | E8 | F2 | ■ |
|----|----|----|----|----|----|----|----|----|----|----|----|----|----|
|    |    | ■ |    | ■ |    |    |    |    |    | ■ |    |    | ■ |

| A4 | H5 | G7 | I11 | I10 | ■ | G3 | H8 | ■ | E3 | ■ | B2 | B1 | D5 | A9 | ■ |
|----|----|----|-----|-----|----|----|----|----|----|----|----|----|----|----|----|
|    |    |    |     |     | ■ |    |    | ■ |    | ■ |    |    |    |    | ■ |

| D4 | C5 | H11 | D9 | D1 | I4 | D6 | E2 | ■ | A10 | C7 | G5 | A6 | D3 | ■ |
|----|----|-----|----|----|----|----|----|----|-----|----|----|----|----|----|
|    |    |     |    |    |    |    |    | ■ |     |    |    |    |    | ■ |

Dear Aunt Mary,

I have stumbled upon a new mystery in
the fabric of the library itself. After
finishing my book on the history of Greenway
- which I will post with this letter, I think
you will find it as fascinating as I did -
I was staring into space when I noticed an
oddity on the wall opposite me. I found a
slightly askew covering for a keyhole, which
I must have knocked out of place earlier as
I was pacing. A door has revealed itself
within the wall, its outlines hidden by the
patterned wallpaper Mrs Ashmore chose.

There is a keyhole, but no key on the
chain the housekeeper had given me when I
first arrived. Surely, if the key was lost
within these walls, I would have found it
by now in my attempts to organise. I sat
at the desk again, feeling increasingly
frustrated. This morning, I spent hours
trying to make sense of the chaos it holds.
Mrs Ashmore has the odd habit of storing
her own replies to letters alongside other
minutiae. One in particular stood out. It is
extremely short - in both length and tone -
with no addressed name:

WE HAVE NO OPENINGS FOR A NEW
LIBRARIAN. I AM QUITE ABLE TO LOOK
AFTER THE GREENWAY LIBRARY BY MYSELF.

REGARDS,

MRS ASHMORE

---

There were numerous scratches on the
well-guarded drawer at the front of the
heavy, wooden structure. But when I went
to open it, the drawer slid out easily. An
old and near-ruined copy of *The Body in the
Library* had been placed inside. Of course,
a similarly creased bundle of pages, folded
underneath the jacket of the hardback book,
was present for me to find.

Mrs Ashmore's puzzles feel like a
lifeline between us, and I must continue to
solve them to get closer to her whereabouts.

Your nephew,

Charles

# LETTER TRAIL

What's the link between these groups?

Which is the odd one out and why?

1.

> B A R B
>
> I D E N T I T Y
>
> H E R
>
> H O L Y

2.

> B L I N D
>
> B R O T H E R
>
> H A Y
>
> Y E T I

3.

BEE

HOLD

RIB

THIN

TRAY

4.

BOY

HID

LABYRINTH

TREE

# CHAPTER 9

# Murder on the Orient Express

THE JOURNEY

ADDER

SNOW STORM

SHADOW QUOTE

TRAIN TRACKS

TRAVELLERS

PIECE TOGETHER

SNOWFLAKES

ALIAS

DEADLY DOZEN

# THE JOURNEY

Follow Hercule Poirot's journey, and that of his fellow passengers, as he leaves Aleppo in Syria bound for London. Some of the places on the way are hidden in the word search grid. Names are in straight lines and can go across, down, forwards, backwards and on any of the diagonals. One name is there twice. Use your own little grey cells to discover what it is . . .

| I | I | S | W | I | T | Z | E | R | L | A | N | D | L | B |
| C | S | N | A | C | N | E | N | E | C | I | N | E | V | U |
| V | T | X | N | T | O | N | I | T | A | L | Y | O | R | D |
| O | A | G | I | S | O | P | P | Z | E | E | S | L | M | A |
| K | N | H | N | D | B | S | A | U | K | T | E | U | R | P |
| N | B | I | N | B | I | R | R | R | A | V | N | P | T | E |
| I | U | O | S | M | N | O | U | I | I | I | S | L | D | S |
| V | L | A | P | A | P | T | V | C | C | S | Y | A | U | T |
| H | A | L | L | E | P | A | A | H | K | O | R | A | A | X |
| U | O | I | A | A | L | L | E | V | L | G | I | A | S | D |
| N | M | L | R | S | A | E | U | I | L | R | A | N | O | E |
| G | R | I | O | I | T | P | I | E | C | N | A | R | F | I |
| A | S | G | S | Q | U | P | B | N | G | Z | B | A | I | V |
| R | U | E | O | S | R | O | S | N | E | M | B | V | A | H |
| Y | N | A | M | R | E | G | N | A | U | S | T | R | I | A |

| | |
|---|---|
| ALEPPO | MILAN |
| ALPS | MUNICH |
| AUSTRIA | PARIS |
| BELGRADE | SIMPLON |
| BROD | SOFIA |
| BUDAPEST | SWITZERLAND |
| CALAIS | SYRIA |
| EUROPE | TURKEY |
| FRANCE | VARNA |
| GERMANY | VENICE |
| HUNGARY | VIENNA |
| INNSBRUCK | VINKOVCI |
| ISTANBUL | YUGOSLAVIA |
| ITALY | ZURICH |
| LONDON | |

# ADDER

Find the answers to each set of clues and join them together to make a new word. You will find the length of the answer words and an additional clue to point you in the right direction.

1.  Gamble (3) + Beam of light (3) =
    Commit an act of treachery (6) _____

2.  Belonging to a lady (3) + Item of jewellery (4) =
    A red one will throw you off the scent! (7) _____

3.  A youngster (3) + A short sleep (3) =
    An abduction (6) _____

4.  Barely, simply (4) + Frozen water (3) =
    Fairness (7) _____

5.  Mark made by a wound to the skin (4) + Rented out (3) =
    Bright red (7) _____

6.  Top of the body (4) + Railway tracks (5) =
    The most important news items (9) _____

7.  However (3) + Heavy weight (3) =
    Fastening on a conductor's uniform (6) _____

8.  Limb (3) + Conclusion (3) =
    A person with a famous reputation — like Poirot! (6)

    _____

# SNOW STORM

A word square reads the same whether going across or down. From the list below, fit four words of four letters into each of the boxes below. Each box must contain the word SNOW.

EWER

IRON

ISLE

LOSE

MISS

NAME

OMEN

SNOW

SNOW

SNOW

SOLO

WENT

# SHADOW QUOTE

Solve the clues and write your answers ACROSS in the larger grid. When this is complete, take the letters in the shaded squares and write them going DOWN in the smaller grid. I have given you the first answer so you might have a chance . . .

When the smaller grid is complete, break the letters into words, which will complete a quotation by Hercule Poirot. It begins, 'The impossible cannot have happened, therefore . . .'

1. Plant which produces leaves used for snuff

2. Leather case for a revolver or for clue 6

3. Travel backwards

4. Almost the same as

5. Spoke very indistinctly

6. Small, hand-held firearms

7. In the open air

8. Inflicted a wound with a knife

9. Person held to ransom

10. Soft indoor shoe

| | | | | | | | |
|---|---|---|---|---|---|---|---|
| 1 | | | | | | | |
| 2 | | | | | | | |
| 3 | | | | | | | |
| 4 | | | | | | | |
| 5 | | | | | | | |
| 6 | | | | | | | |
| 7 | | | | | | | |
| 8 | | | | | | | |
| 9 | | | | | | | |
| 10 | | | | | | | |

| 1 | 2 | 3 | 4 | 5 | 6 | 7 | 8 | 9 | 10 |
|---|---|---|---|---|---|---|---|---|---|
| T | | | | | | | | | |
| B | | | | | | | | | |
| O | | | | | | | | | | |

# TRAIN TRACKS

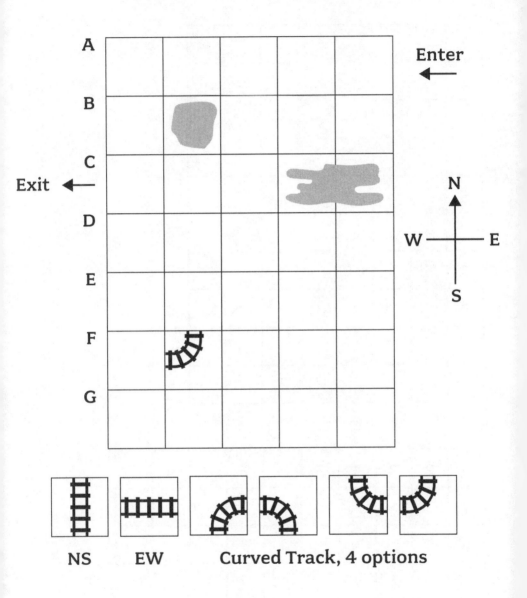

NS    EW    Curved Track, 4 options

Plot the position of the rail tracks through the snowclad landscape. Enter in the direction indicated, top right. The railway exits in the direction shown at the first square in row C on the left.

SIX different types of track can be used:

NS. Running North to South.

EW. Running East to West.

CURVED. There are FOUR options for these, as shown.

There are areas showing frozen lakes in both rows B and C. These cannot be crossed by rail tracks.

**Row A uses: 1 Curved**
**Row B uses: 2 Curved + 1 EW**
**Row C uses: 3 Curved**
**Row D uses: 2 Curved + 1 NS + 2 EW**
**Row E uses: 4 Curved + 1 NS**
**Row F uses: 2 Curved + 3 NS**
**Row G uses: 4 Curved + 1 EW**

One piece of track is already in place in row F.

**Can you follow the plan and plot the path of the rail tracks?**

# TRAVELLERS

As you will know, Agatha Christie was fascinated by the Orient Express and enjoyed many rail trips. One such experience — an incident when a train was snowbound for six days — sparked her imagination to create a backdrop for her murder mystery novel set on a train trapped by the snow.

Here we have different travellers on board the Orient Express. Each person has a different profession and boarded the train at a different location. During a temporary halt in their journey caused by a giant snowdrift, they exchange stories. They have all travelled before on the train and experienced delays because of the snow. Can you match all the details together in the travellers' tales?

Use the information below so that you can fill in the larger grid. When you find a piece of positive information, put a tick in the correct box. Put a cross when you have found a piece of negative information. Cross-refer until you can complete the box at the foot of the page.

## CLUES

1. The detective was once delayed by snow for twice the hours that Mr Ryton had been.
2. Miss Worrall boarded at Venice. She was fascinated to hear that the journalist was once delayed for 20 hours by the weather.
3. Mr Parker, a lawyer, boarded at Paris, while the person who got on at Belgrade recalled a delay of 4 hours.
4. The person who once had an 8-hour delay got on the train at Sofia.
5. The musician recalled how she was once snowbound for 12 hours.
6. Mrs Kravitz did not board the train at Sofia.

|  | PROFESSION | | | | | BOARDED | | | | | SNOWBOUND | | | | |
|---|---|---|---|---|---|---|---|---|---|---|---|---|---|---|---|
| | Detective | Journalist | Lawyer | Musician | Teacher | Paris | Milan | Venice | Belgrade | Sofia | 4 hours | 8 hours | 12 hours | 16 hours | 20 hours |
| **NAME** Miss Worrall | | | | | | | | | | | | | | | |
| Mr Delaney | | | | | | | | | | | | | | | |
| Mr Ryton | | | | | | | | | | | | | | | |
| Mrs Kravitz | | | | | | | | | | | | | | | |
| Mr Parker | | | | | | | | | | | | | | | |
| **SNOWBOUND** 4 hours | | | | | | | | | | | | | | | |
| 8 hours | | | | | | | | | | | | | | | |
| 12 hours | | | | | | | | | | | | | | | |
| 16 hours | | | | | | | | | | | | | | | |
| 20 hours | | | | | | | | | | | | | | | |
| **BOARDED** Paris | | | | | | | | | | | | | | | |
| Milan | | | | | | | | | | | | | | | |
| Venice | | | | | | | | | | | | | | | |
| Belgrade | | | | | | | | | | | | | | | |
| Sofia | | | | | | | | | | | | | | | |

| NAME | PROFESSION | BOARDED | SNOWBOUND |
|---|---|---|---|
| | | | |
| | | | |
| | | | |
| | | | |
| | | | |

# PIECE TOGETHER

**Can you fit all the listed names into the grid?** Words read either across or down. There is only one possible solution. To make it even trickier, there is one listed word that does NOT appear in the grid.

## 4 LETTERS

BOUC
JOHN
MARY

## 5 LETTERS

CYRUS
DAISY
ELENA
GRETA
HENRY
SONIA

## 6 LETTERS

HECTOR
ORIENT
PIERRE
POIROT
SAMUEL

## 7 LETTERS

ANTONIO
EXPRESS
HARDMAN
HERCULE
NATALIA
RUDOLPH
SCHMIDT

## 8 LETTERS

CAROLINE
CASSETTI
DEBENHAM
MACQUEEN
RATCHETT

## 9 LETTERS

ARBUTHNOT
ARMSTRONG
MASTERMAN

## 10 LETTERS

FOSCARELLI
HILDEGARDE

## 11 LETTERS

CONSTANTINE

# SNOWFLAKES

The journey of the Orient Express through central Europe was delayed due to a snowdrift. In this puzzle, you must solve the clues and slot the answers into their correct places in the snowflake grids. **But which snowflake?**

The clues are in no particular order. The answer to clue 1-2 in the top grid is **KNIFE** and the answer to 1-2 in the lower grid is **CHILD**. **Where do the rest of the answers go?**

**CLUES**

- Cutting tool or weapon

- Young person, like Daisy Armstrong

- Take place

- Bunk on a ship or railway carriage

- Timepiece

- Railway conductor

- Hours of darkness

- A sleeping car, a _ _ _ _ _ -lit

- Frequently

- Aristocratic title of Rudolph Andrenyi

- Water vapour which would power a locomotive

- A means of transport such as the Orient Express!

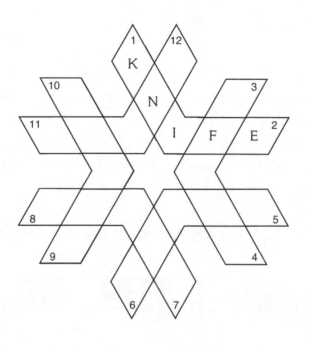

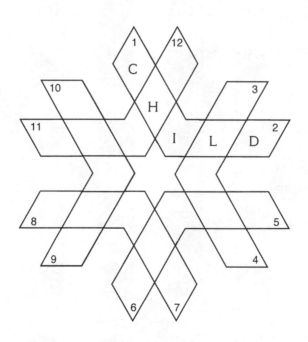

# ALIAS

Some passengers on the Orient Express are known, or have been known, by an alias. Much like me, they are not always who they appear to be.

The same can be said for the words in this crossword. The clue is an anagram of its answer, the same letters are used, but in a different order to make a different word. Watch out! Sometimes a clue word can form different new words and then a choice has to be made. There's only one way to complete the grid.

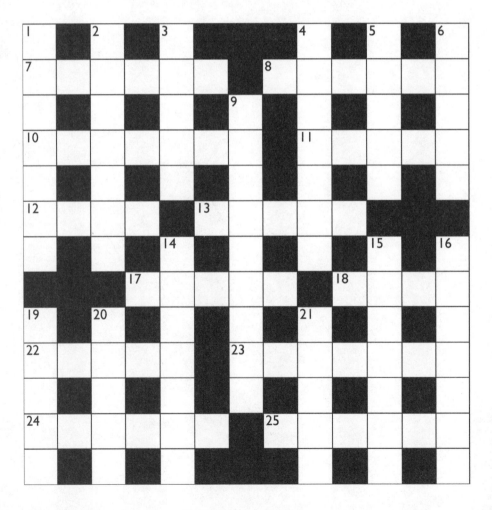

## ACROSS

7   Manors
8   Asleep
10  Rattles
11  Agree
12  Dame
13  Alert
17  Bairn
18  Cone
22  Grown
23  Corsets
24  Desire
25  Lanced

## DOWN

1   Supreme
2   Draws on
3   Outer
4   Peelers
5   Anger
6   Share
9   Versatile
14  Gyrated
15  Untried
16  Defeats
19  Worse
20  Boats
21  Canoe

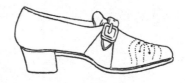

# DEADLY DOZEN

Poirot considers the possibility that there might be more than one murderer aboard the Orient Express. Here are EIGHT further crimes. **How many people were involved in each one?**

The clue is the number hidden in each sentence. The number is written out as a word appearing as a continuous line of letters, split between existing words.

**CLUES**

1.  Their weapon of choice was a chisel, even though it was rather a clumsy tool to carry around.

2.  As a dilemma, you couldn't make it worse, as the accused had no credible alibi.

3.  In their haste nothing was properly checked at the crime scene.

4.  The assassins' eventual victim was unaware of their stealthy approach.

5.  'If our plan works,' they said, 'we shall be rich beyond our wildest dreams!'

6.  The plotters took the same train on each day of the week to become familiar with the route.

7. The confusion in each case, with so many involved, was difficult for the detectives to solve.

8. The fraudster told his accomplices, 'We can obtain the cash, if I verify the signatures.'

Dear Aunt Mary,

The police have arrived.

Knowing a key must be present somewhere for this secret door, and that Mrs Ashmore had a habit of hiding things in odd places, I looked to the sliding cabinets closest to the door's outline. I spied a book that had been put on the shelf the wrong way around, the spine facing the wall instead of outwards into the room. I tried to grip it and pull it free, sliding out a corner of a special edition of *Murder on the Orient Express*. Pulling it again further produced both a click and a bundle of puzzles to fall free.

And so the room was revealed, with poor Mrs Ashmore inside.

The police have now fully taken over, of course, with detectives questioning the staff. They have found no clues as to who would have motive to murder Mrs Ashmore. Indeed, she is not well liked in the house. The cook described her as fussy, the handyman wasn't ever allowed in the room, the house manager had no time for her. All in the house had the opportunity to commit the crime, but none truly stand out, at least to me, as hating Mrs Ashmore so much as to murder her.

I am yet to tell them of the puzzles Mrs Ashmore left behind. If only I could see them spread out together, I am sure they will reveal the answer.

I do fear I must leave the conclusion to this mystery in the hands of the detectives who know best. Before I make my way to the local station, though, I must at least attempt the very last puzzle she left me. I found it clutched in her hand when I stumbled upon her in that secret room.

Your nephew,

Charles

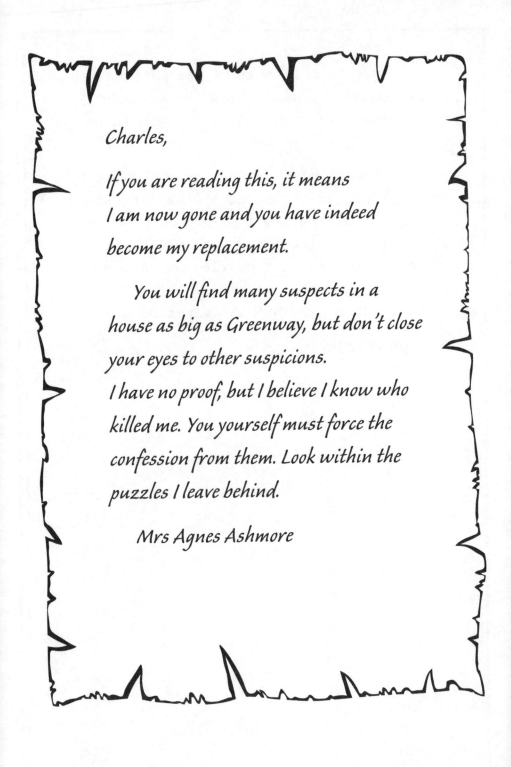

Charles,

If you are reading this, it means
I am now gone and you have indeed
become my replacement.

You will find many suspects in a
house as big as Greenway, but don't close
your eyes to other suspicions.
I have no proof, but I believe I know who
killed me. You yourself must force the
confession from them. Look within the
puzzles I leave behind.

Mrs Agnes Ashmore

# ALL SHALL BE REVEALED

If you have solved my puzzles correctly, you
will be able to find the twelve letters below.

## IN DISGUISE (p.20)

Of all the letters replaced by a black square,
this one comes last alphabetically.

_____

## DOING THE ROUNDS (p.40)

There is one letter pair left over when the
puzzle is finished. What are the letters?

_____ _____

RETURN JOURNEY (p.62)

What are the letters in the shaded squares?

____   ____   ____

HONEY POT (p.86)

What is the letter immediately to the

left of the number 3, and the letter

immediately to the right of number 8?

____   ____

DOUBLE DEAL (p.106)

What is the one letter of the alphabet that

does not appear in any of the answers?

____

*MOVING ON (p.127)*

*What is the middle letter of the missing word?*

_____

*VOWEL PLAY (p.148)*

*What vowel appears the least number*

*of times once the grid is complete?*

_____

*LETTER TRAIL (p.168)*

*Which letter is missing from the*

*anagram of group 3?*

_____

*Arrange the deadly dozen and all will be revealed.*

Dear Charles,

I write this note to ask your forgiveness.

I can hardly imagine how bewildering it has been for you to come to work at such a magnificent house and as fascinating a place as Greenway, only to have been met with such a strange reception.

You are an intelligent young man but, having watched you grow all these years, I truly believed a little push was all that was necessary to secure your first role. I wrote to Mrs Ashmore several times over the past few months, with no reply forthcoming. If she truly was a good person, she surely would have written back. And I would have stopped adding the thallium to the letters I sent her.

Each letter contained only a very low dose, just to test her. Surely, as a fellow fan of Agatha Christie, she should have been expecting some sort of retribution for her behaviour . . .

I didn't think contact with the poison was going to drive her steadily mad, and I never meant to kill her either. Indeed, when she finally did reply - sending me that short, clipped letter - I was at first pleased.

But on hearing that you didn't stand a chance to fill the role I knew you would be perfect for, I had to step in. I went to visit her - and supply the antidote, of course - but she was just as rude in person as she was in her letter.

What could I do but create an opportunity for you, dear Charles? She hid in that secret room of hers, but by then it was too late. I realised on seeing her that I'd accidentally supplied Mrs Ashmore with so much of the poison, she wouldn't last much longer anyway.

I sat down at her desk and wrote one final letter, inviting you to Greenway as its new and *rightful* librarian.

It was only on receipt of more and more puzzles from you that I realised she was up to something, even now.

I stopped replying to you in the hope that you wouldn't be able to complete the conundrums, which I was sure would eventually spell out my doom.

I hear the sirens now, and write this last note to you to explain my actions. I have embroiled you in a mystery like those of our beloved Agatha Christie.

I hope you can forgive me, in time.

Your Aunt Mary

# ANSWERS

## CHAPTER 1:
## THE MYSTERIOUS AFFAIR AT STYLES

### THE GREAT DETECTIVE

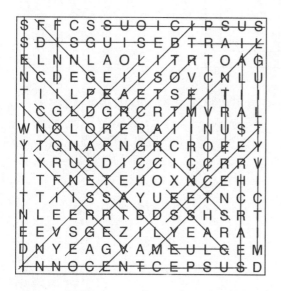

The unused letters in the first four columns spell out 'LITTLE GREY CELLS'.

### CONNECTING ROOMS

You end up in John Cavendish's room. You did not inspect Alfred Inglethorp's room. You started off in the spare room adjacent to the bathroom.

# SECRET CODE

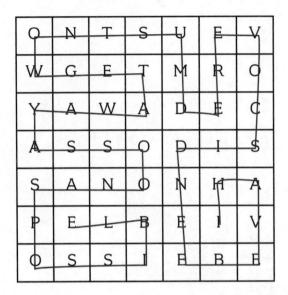

The message reads: *I have been discovered. Must now get away as soon as possible.*

## PIECE TOGETHER

The message reads: *I suspect my husband of fraud. What can I do?*

## MAKE A WILL

**Grid A:** 1 Make, 2 Rake, 3 Rate, 4 Rote, 5 Rots, 6 Rats, 7 Mats, 8 Mate.
**Grid B:** 1 Will, 2 Wall, 3 Wail, 4 Wait, 5 Bait, 6 Bail, 7 Ball, 8 Bill.

## ACTING ON INSTINCT

1 Executor, 2 Hospital, 3 Hastings, 4 Poisoned, 5 Medicine,
6 Narrator, 7 Baffling, 8 Uniforms, 9 Fragment, 10 Renowned.

*'Instinct is a marvellous thing,'* mused Poirot. *'It can neither be . . . explained nor ignored.'*

# POISONED CRYPTIC

*Across:* 3 Match, 7 Beauty, 8 Evelyn, 10 **Strychnine**, 11 Liar, 12 Stone, 13 Prosecute, 16 Mission, 21 M**onkshood**, 22 Trays, 23 Will, 24 Evergreens, 26 Friend, 27 Blinds, 28 Stove.
*Down:* 1 Testate, 2 Buoyant, 3 Myth, 4 Here, 5 **Hemlock**, 6 Dynasty, 9 Microscopes, 14 Stop, 15 Rich, 17 Topiary, 18 Skillet, 19 **Arsenic**, 20 **Cyanide**, 24 Ends, 25 Gibe.

# CANDLELIGHT

The order is: 10, 6, 8, 4, 7, 1, 5, 3, 9, 2. Candle number 4 was the fourth to be picked up. This is the only instance when the number on the candle matches the number in order that the candle was picked up.

# COMME ÇA

A few words in the sentences sound just like numbers in French. The dates are 15th May, 20th June and 16th July.

1. I need to know what happened to those petrol <u>cans</u>. If the boat <u>sank</u> I would never forgive myself.
   *Cans* sounds like quinze, which is 15. *Sank* sounds like cinq which is 5. 15/5 is 15th May.

2. The brake <u>van</u> could be found at the rear of the train as a safety feature. Accidents may not <u>cease</u>, but may be reduced.
   *Van* sounds like vingt, which is 20. *Cease* sounds like six which is 6. 20/6 is 20th June.

3. The doctor <u>says</u> that all is now going well. He is all <u>set</u> to discharge the patient without further delay.
   *Says* sounds like seize, which is 16. *Set* sounds like sept, which is 7. 16/7 is 16th July.

# ALL ABOUT STYLES

```
S     H     S C O T L A N D Y A R D           W
T     J A P P         E             R       I I
E     S     I     B A U E R S T E I N       G D
P     T     R   D   S     E   H       G   O
M E D I C I N E   T     F E U D   L A W
O     N     T   A   W     U   R       E
T     G     L E T H A L   G           T     C
H     S     A   H   Y   B E A R D     H     O
E   F M         S       E       E     O     U
R   R P A N     C       E       T     R     N
  W I L L       B O T T L E     E     P     T
    E     C     T       S   C           R
C Y N T H I A   S T Y L E S T T M A R Y
U   D   E   V   A   I   E   I   L     M
P       R   E   G   B O X   V   F     A
S T R Y C H N I N E     R       E   R   N
      U   D     M A R Y         E     O
  E X P L A I N   A   R     P O W D E R
      E   S       S P Y         A
      H   K       P O I R O T
```

# IN DISGUISE

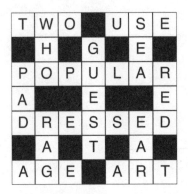

# CHAPTER 2:
# THE MURDER AT THE VICARAGE

## TELEPHONE EXCHANGE

The numbers translated to letters spell out the warning message:
*The iced cake may make you ill.*

## LOSING THE PLOT

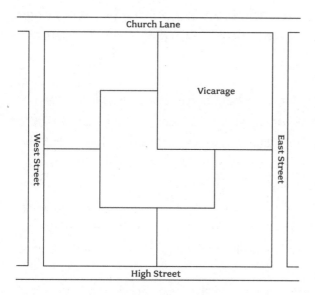

## QUOTE LINES

1 Garden, 2 Fan, 3 Wealthy, 4 Fuel, 5 Tennis, 6 Portrait, 7 Tip, 8 Coy, 9 Shine, 10 Handsome.

The quotation reads: *'There is no detective in England equal to a spinster lady of uncertain age with plenty of time on her hands.'*

# GOSSIP

First Anne. Second Mary. Third Lawrence. Fourth Colonel. Fifth Lettice. Sixth Dennis. Seventh Griselda.

The three lists contain twenty-one names (3 x 7). As each lady has placed three names correctly, that means nine names are in the correct place (3 x 3). The seven visitors have all been placed correctly at least once. Take this number away from the total number of correctly placed people (9 − 7 = 2). There are two names which appear in more than one list, and they must be in their correct places.  Lettice and Griselda are the only names appearing twice in the same order.  Lettice was the fifth caller and Griselda the seventh.

That being so, Mary cannot have been fifth, and the Colonel can be discounted from being seventh. Three names were written down for the person making the sixth call. Griselda and Lettice have already been accounted for, so they can be dismissed. From the first to the seventh caller, there was no instance where all the three ladies got all the names wrong. With two names discounted, the third caller has to be the only name left. That is Dennis. His name can be crossed off in both Mrs Price-Ridley and Miss Hartnell's selection.

Miss Weatherby has correctly named the fifth, sixth and seventh caller. As each lady correctly identified three callers, her choices for first, second, third and fourth callers must be incorrect. From here, using the process of elimination, we are led to the final and correct list.

## HYMN NUMBERS

The final hymn will be hymn number 073 (seventy-three). The pattern is based on the number of letters in the numbers when they are written out as words.

013 (thirteen) is the lowest number to contain eight letters.
017 (seventeen) is the lowest number to contain nine letters.
024 (twenty-four) is the lowest number to contain ten letters.
023 (twenty-three) is the lowest number to contain eleven letters.

The next number in the sequence is the lowest number to contain twelve letters, and that is 073 (seventy-three).

## WORD LADDER

*Ladder 1*: 1 Slack, 2 Slick, 3 Slice, 4 Slide, 5 Glide, 6 Guide.
*Ladder 2*: 1 Slack, 2 Shack, 3 Shark, 4 Share, 5 Shore, 6 Chore.

## GRAVESTONES

1 Poisoned, 2 Drowning, 3 Smothered, 4 Strangled, 5 Bludgeoned, 6 Suffocated, 7 Stabbed, 8 Asphyxiated.

## BEAT THE CLOCK

*Clock 1*: 11 seconds. Twelve is double six (it is tempting to double the 5 seconds and give 10 as an answer). The first two strikes would only take 1 second.

*Clock 2*: Six days. There are twenty-four hours in a day (5 x 24 = 120 minutes). The clock loses 120 minutes — or two hours — per day. In six days, it will have lost twelve hours and the time will be accurate.

## DOUBLE CROSS

*Across*: 1 School, 4 Temper, 9 Rarer, 10 Trebles, 11 Bloomer, 13 Utter, 14 Spring, 15 Pickle, 18 China, 20 Tangent, 22 Edition, 23 Cairn, 24 Digest, 25 Ledger.
*Down*: 1 Scrub, 2 Harbour, 3 Oar, 5 Execution, 6 Pilot, 7 Reserve, 8 Start, 12 Mandarins, 14 Succeed, 16 Keeping, 17 Stone, 19 Icing, 21 Tenor, 23 Cue.

## THE CURATE'S COLLECTION

The total was £4 6s (four pounds, six shillings).

Mrs Price-Ridley put in a pound. Two people put in 5 shillings each and two people put in two half-crowns each, which makes four lots of 5 shillings which is a further pound. Three people put in twice the total of two half-crowns, i.e. ten shillings each, making thirty shillings. There was one ten-shilling note which, added to thirty shillings makes another forty shillings, so another two pounds. Finally, the four sixpences make two shillings, and each florin is worth two shillings, making six shillings in all.

The grand total was therefore four pounds six shillings (before the £1 note disappeared!).

## DOING THE ROUNDS

1 Ether, 2 Erase, 3 Seize, 4 Zebra, 5 Rally, 6 Lynch, 7 Chafe, 8 Feast, 9 Stain, 10 Inset.

# CHAPTER 3:
# 4.50 FROM PADDINGTON

## POINTS EAST

1 Bell, 2 Port, 3 Stock, 4 Stop, 5 Trip, 6 Car.

## THE CARRIAGE MURDER

A5 was the carriage where the murder took place.

A1 Four ladies
A2 Miss Piggot
A3 Reverend Batty
A4 Lady Pearl
A5 The gentleman and the unfortunate lady
A6 Colonel Upshot
A7 Four ladies

The group of eight ladies could not have been further apart in the first-class section, so they occupied A1 and A7. Reverend Batty half-remembered he was in an odd-numbered carriage. It wasn't 1 or 7 so must have been 3 or 5. Colonel Upshot avoided Batty and left two carriages before boarding. This means Batty could not have been in A5 and must have been in A3. That places Upshot in A6. Miss Piggot was next to Reverend Batty, so she must have been in either A2 or A4. Lady Pearl said there was a gentleman either side of her, which would not be the case if Miss Piggot was in carriage A4. Lady Pearl was on her own, so she could not be in the carriage adjacent to Colonel Upshot, where there was arguing. Lady Pearl must be in A4. The arguing couple were in A5: the scene of the crime!

# SEARCHING FOR SUSTENANCE

The unused letters spell out the word **CRACKERS**.

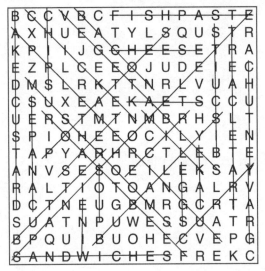

## FESTIVE SYMBOLS

1 Bells, 2 Baubles, 3 Angel, 4 Tinsel, 5 Tree, 6 Garland, 7 Lights,
8 Paper Chains.

## STATION-ARY

There are sixteen stations on the map. There is one that you cannot
reach without doubling back.

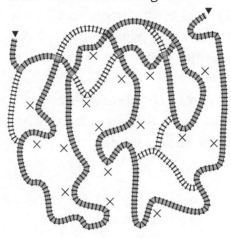

## MISS MARPLE PRESCRIBES

1 Magazine, 2 Villages, 3 Scissors, 4 Confetti, 5 Mahogany,
6 Executor, 7 Wireless, 8 Holidays, 9 Powerful, 10 Figurine.

Miss Marple prescribes *'a glass of my cowslip wine'*.

## SPOKES

1 Make-up, 2 Poison, 3 Kettle, 4 Powder, 5 Harold, 6 Police, 7 Cajole,
8 Potato, 9 Studio, 10 Misers, 11 Sponge, 12 Fridge.

## UNCOUPLING

*Across*: 7 Animal, 8 Barrel, 10 Stretch, 11 Stand, 12 Girl, 13 Linen,
17 Cloth, 18 Shoe, 22 Press, 23 Account, 24 Carpet, 25 Father.
*Down*: 1 Sausage, 2 Library, 3 Party, 4 Parsley, 5 Cream, 6 Slide,
9 Christmas, 14 Plaster, 15 Thought, 16 Letters, 19 Space, 20 Heart,
21 Ocean.

## TIMETABLE

At Carvil Junction, no ladies or gentlemen got off, but three
gentlemen got on. Paddington had twelve passengers in first:
four ladies and eight gentlemen. Leaving Brackhampton, there
were six ladies and three gentlemen. There was no change at
Waverton. Arriving at Carvil Junction, there were six ladies and
three gentlemen. Of these, three ladies and three gentlemen were
staying on to go to Roxeter. There needed to be the same number
of passengers who left Paddington, so three gentlemen must have
boarded at Carvil Junction.

# BACK ON TRACK

Coal truck, Dining car, Guard's van, Mail coach, Milk train.

# RETURN JOURNEY

```
        B               R E F R E S H M E N T S       N
    B U F F E T         A                       E     O
      S   I   O   S     I       S       S       R     N
      Y   R O U T E     L O C O M O T I V E S         S
          S   R   A     W   E   A   E   E     E       T
      S   T   I   T R A I N L I N E S           O
  C L O C K S       Y   I   L   R       M A P
      E   L   T   S   C   C       D       E
      E   A       I   A       C   I   H E L P
      P A S S E N G E R T R A I N       T   A
      E   S   A   N   R   B   I   S         S
      R   T       I   B   E N G I N E S     A
  U S E   C   S   A   U   G   T           A
        B O O K I N G O F F I C E     B A G
  T E A   R   N   E   F   A       A   E
  E       R   G       D E P A R T U R E
  N   W H I S T L E     R   I   R   R
  D A   D   E   A   S   S T A T I O N
  E I   O       S   L   C   E
  R E T U R N T I C K E T   E   K   R U N
```

# CHAPTER 4:
# A MURDER IS ANNOUNCED

## CRYPTIC

*Across*: 1 Cashed, 4 Tables, 9 India, 10 Handles, 11 Article, 13 Uncle, 14 Ordeal, 15 Scored, 18 Carol, 20 Paddock, 22 Adapted, 23 Petal, 24 Dimmed, 25 Spares.
*Down*: 1 China, 2 Sedated, 3 Era, 5 Announced, 6 Lilac, 7 Suspend, 8 Chief, 12 Charlotte, 14 Orchard, 16 Rooster, 17 Spade, 19 Realm, 21 Kills, 23 Pip.

## THE ANNOUNCEMENT

A The visitor is the moon.
B Silence will be broken by the chime of the clock at 6.30 p.m.
C Inaccurately.
D A coffin.

## SWITCHED IDENTITY

ACES — CASE, DALES — LEADS, DANGER — GARDEN,
ESTRANGE — SERGEANT, FINDERS — FRIENDS, HATED — DEATH,
HATTER — THREAT, HECTORS — TORCHES, HIRE — HEIR,
HOST — SHOT, ITEM — TIME, LOVES — SOLVE, MOOR — ROOM,
MUCH — CHUM, OLIVETS — VIOLETS, ORIENTAL — RELATION,
PALER — PEARL, PART — TRAP, PECTINS — INSPECT,
RAWNESS — ANSWERS, RED RUM — MURDER, RESIST — SISTER,
SAVE — VASE, SEASIDE — DISEASE, SKILL — KILLS,
SLIVER — SILVER, SOOTHING — SHOOTING, SPOILT — PISTOL,
SPOON — SNOOP, STARVED — ADVERTS, TEA SET — ESTATE,
TESTING — SETTING, TUNA — AUNT, VERSATILE — RELATIVES.

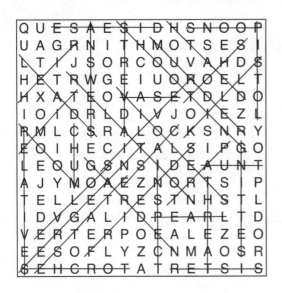

## SEPARATED

1 Asp + Ire = Aspire, 2 Ban + King = Banking,
3 Band + Age = Bandage, 4 Cap + Size = Capsize,
5 Cut + Lass = Cutlass, 6 Imp + Rove = Improve,
7 Pan + Ache = Panache, 8 Pat + Riot = Patriot,
9 Ram + Parts = Ramparts, 10 Sup + Port = Support.

## RATIONING

A Eggs, B Tea, C Meat, D Butter, E Margarine, F Sweets,
G Currants, H Cheese.

# NEGATIVE

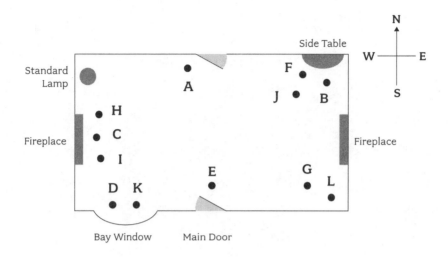

## PRAISE INDEED

1 Scotland, 2 Valuable, 3 Rationed, 4 Identity, 5 Shepherd,
6 Poisoned, 7 Revolver, 8 Nickname, 9 Gardener, 10 Refugees.

Quote: 'She's just the finest detective God ever made.'
The character with this opinion is retired detective (Sir Henry)
Clithering. He is of course describing Miss Marple.

## FLY THE FLAG

1 Channel, 2 Lucerne, 3 Austria, 4 Anthems, 5 Cheeses, 6 Georgia,
7 Iceland, 8 Strauss, 9 Spanish, 10 Gondola, 11 Russian.

The central shaded area spells out **NETHERLANDS**.

## DELICIOUS DEATH

The missing ingredient is **RUM**.

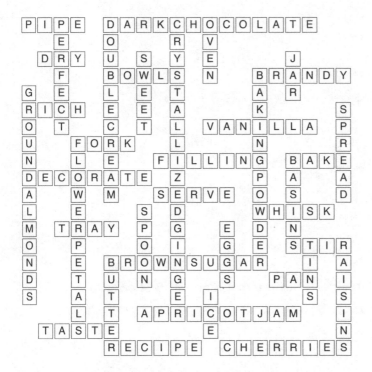

## NAME CHECK

1 Amy, 2 Rudi, 3 Dora, 4 Pip, 5 Jane.

## HONEY POT

C = Clockwise, A = Anticlockwise

1. C Market, 2. A Archie, 3. C Choker, 4. A Revoke, 5. A Dinner,
6. C Invite, 7. C Target, 8. A Garden, 9. A Deduce, 10. C Police,
11. C Exiles, 12. C Estate

# CHAPTER 5:
# THE ABC MURDERS

## ALPHA CODE

*Across (left to right, top to bottom):* Lawyer, Question, Stab, Voice, Tied, Devon, Overcoats, Teashop, Passers by, Razor, Area, Eject, Robs, Asterisk, Little.
*Down (top to bottom, left to right):* Waitress, Arrest, Eyebrow, Escaped, Drove, Gear, Exit, Invisible, Fete, Room, Stole, Station, Narrate, Moment, Doorbell.

1 = D, 2 = E, 3 = V, 4 = O, 5 = N, 6 = S, 7 = A, 8 = I, 9 = T, 10 = C, 11 = W, 12 = B, 13 = M, 14 = F, 15 = Q, 16 = G, 17 = R, 18 = H, 19 = J, 20 = U, 21 = Z, 22 = X, 23 = L, 24 = K, 25 = P, 26 = Y.

**JIGSAW** is the name of the toy. Poirot likens this to an investigation where everyone involved is a piece of a jigsaw.

## LAST LIST

1 Great Yarmouth, 2 Ilfracombe, 3 Faversham, 4 Eastbourne, 5 Kettering, 6 Maidstone, 7 Lancaster, 8 Harrogate, 9 Jarrow.

## TRUE TO TYPE

Typewriter 3 wrote the message.

## GONE MISSING

1 Tablecloth, 2 Diabetic, 3 Fabric, 4 Abscond, 5 Abduction, 6 Roadblock, 7 Abstinence, 8 Absence.

## NINE LIVES

1 Cat (The Ginger Cat Café), 2 Treason, 3 Code.
The location is **DONCASTER**, where murder number four was committed.


## WORD PLAY

1 Luggage, 2 Station, 3 Letters, 4 Brother, 5 Seaside, 6 Forgery, 7 Chatter, 8 Coaches.

The quotation by Poirot to Megan Barnard is: *'Words, mademoiselle, are only . . . the outer clothing of ideas.'*


## HOAX?

The message reads: A card arrived in the last post. On balance, the coach crash can be called an accident as claimed.


## WHERE AM I?

**RIPON.** The first letter could be an E, M or R. The second letter has to be I, and the third letter has to be P. The fourth letter could be an O or P. The last letter has to be N.  The only combination to make a place is **RIPON.** As in murder D in *The ABC Murders*, there's a horse racing link.

## ALPHABET CROSSWORD

*Across*: 7 Killed, 9 Unrest, 10 Outwitting, 11 Xmas, 12 Reply,
13 Constable, 15 Widower, 20 Firelight, 21 Get up, 23 Jail,
24 Nectarines, 25 Zither, 26 Donald.
*Down*: 1 Minutes, 2 Ill will, 3 Edits, 4 Suggested, 5 Brixham,
6 Assault, 8 Philosophical, 14 Visionary, 16 Titanic, 17 Healthy,
18 Lenient, 19 Quietly, 22 Yards.

Alphabetical order of answers: Assault, Brixham, Constable, Donald,
Edits, Firelight, Get up, Healthy, Ill will, Jail, Killed, Lenient, Minutes,
Nectarines, Outwitting, Philosophical, Quietly, Reply, Suggested,
Titanic, Unrest, Visionary, Widower, Xmas, Yards, Zither.

## LINKS

Messages 1, 2, 3 and 4 can be made just using the letters in the top
row of a QWERTY typewriter. Message 5 needs the L, A and D from
the second row.

## DOUBLE DEAL

Across: 1 Accused, 7 Megan, 8 Traffic, 9 Tempts, 11 Pilot, 13 Fame,
14 Equator, 15 Dawn, 16 In law, 17 Alcove, 21 Ukulele, 22 Alice,
23 Spanish

Down: 2 Carmichael, 3 Unfrozen, 4 Exit, 5 Fete, 6 Japp, 9 Truth,
10 Timetables, 12 Guide, 13 Franklin, 18 Calm, 19 Vice, 20 Skip

The letter that does not appear in any of the answers: Y

# CHAPTER 6:
# DEAD MAN'S FOLLY

## AT THE FÊTE

**FOLLY** appears three times and **SKITTLES** doesn't appear at all.

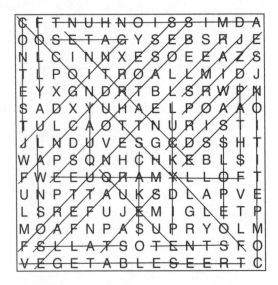

## HOOPLA

*Hoop A*: 1 Stage, 2 Genre, 3 Recap, 4 Apple, 5 Legal, 6 Alias, 7 Aster, 8 Erica, 9 Catch, 10 Chest.

*Hoop B*: 1 Serve, 2 Vetch, 3 Chime, 4 Metal, 5 Alter, 6 Erode, 7 Deuce, 8 Cedar, 9 Arena, 10 Nasse.

## TRUE FOLLY

The thirteenth word, which won't fit into the grid, is **MURDERS**.

# WATER-WAYS

1 Ford, Lake, 2 Loch, Mere, 3 Brook, Canal, 4 Creek, Ocean, 5 Firth, Reach, 6 Marsh, River, 7 Lagoon, Stream, 8 Channel, Estuary.

# YHA

The tastes of the YHA backpackers reflect their support for the YHA, where the initials of its name all have vertical symmetry. The two halves of the letters in the words are mirror images of each other when seen as capital letters.

# JUST THE OPPOSITE

*Across*: 7 Exited, 8 Leader, 10 Fragile, 11 Large, 12 Care, 13 Right, 17 Timid, 18 Nude, 22 Extra, 23 Unearth, 24 Expert, 25 Asleep.
*Down*: 1 Perfect, 2 Bizarre, 3 Peril, 4 Wealthy, 5 Adore, 6 Order, 9 Delicious, 14 Rivalry, 15 Hurried, 16 Perhaps, 19 Level, 20 Stops, 21 Tense.

# WORD WALL

Three words remain: **EGG SHAPED HEAD**.
Anagrams of each other: manor, Norma, Roman.
Hair colours: auburn, blonde, grey.
A boating link: ferry, helm, oar, wheel.
Words that rhyme with a word meaning destiny: fate, which rhymes with fête, plate, wait.
Names associated with helping Poirot: former colleague (Arthur) Hastings, secretary Miss Lemon.
Mrs Oliver's favourite fruit: apples.
Poirot's London telephone exchange: Trafalgar.

# RAFFLE WINNERS

First prize: pig / ticket 183 / Miss Joy Pollitt.
Second prize: fruit hamper / ticket 111 / Julie Brewer.
Third prize: rose bush / ticket 222/ Adam Ploughman.
Fourth prize: cake / ticket 289 / Matt Hands.
Fifth prize: doll / ticket 308 / the verger.

# GARDENS AND GROUNDS

| 1 | 2 |   | 1 |   | B | 2 | B | 1 |
|---|---|---|---|---|---|---|---|---|
| B |   | B |   |   |   |   |   |   |
|   |   |   | B |   | B |   |   | B |
| B | 2 | B |   |   | 4 |   |   | 2 |
|   |   |   | B |   | B | 2 | B |   |
| B |   | B |   |   |   |   |   |   |
| 1 |   |   | 3 | B |   | B |   | 1 |
|   |   | B |   | 1 | 3 |   |   | B |
|   | 1 |   |   |   | 1 | B | 2 |   |

# JIGSAW PIECES

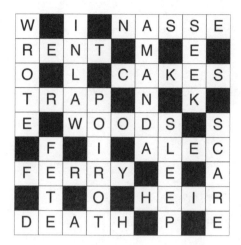

## MOVING ON

**Ovals** is the missing word. Look at word four and word eight in each statement. In 4, take the word BANJO and move on every letter four places in the alphabet. B becomes F, A becomes E and so on to create the eighth word. In 5 the letters in the fourth word move forward five places to make the eighth word. In 6 the letters in the fourth word move forward six places to make the eighth word. In 7 the letters in the fourth word need to move forward seven places to make the eighth word. H becomes O, O becomes V and so on.

# CHAPTER 7:
# DEATH ON THE NILE

## PUZZLING PYRAMID

1 Carl, 2 Plan, 3 Area, 4 Knew, 5 Rare, 6 Dear, 7 Awry, 8 Peer,
9 Free, 10 Fake.

## WHO SAID THAT?

1 Mothers, 2 Rambles, 3 Fortune, 4 Explore, 5 Rattled, 6 Glitter,
7 Unearth, 8 Student, 9 Outside, 10 Neither.

The quotation was spoken by **MR FERGUSON**. He said, *'It is not
the past that matters, but the future.'* These words were first
spoken in **LUXOR**.

## HIEROGLYPHICS

1 **PEARLS**, 2 **OPALS**, 3 **SAPPHIRES**, 4 **LAPIS LAZULI**, 5 **RUBIES**.

## BURIAL CHAMBERS

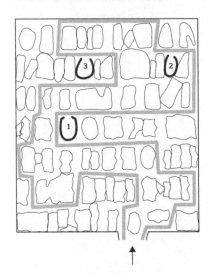

## TRIPLICATIONS

1 Neil, Line, Nile, 2 Andrew, Wander, Warned, 3 Parle, Pearl, Paler, 4 Garden, Ranged, Danger, 5 Tales, Steal, Least, 6 Shire, Heirs, Hires, 7 Steam, Teams, Mates.

## INTERLOCKED

1 Travel, 2 Lethal, 3 Calais, 4 Francs, 5 Aegean, 6 Greece, 7 Ascend, 8 Madame, 9 Esteem, 10 Tongue, 11 Laughs, 12 Pearls.

## BACK TO FRONT

1 Recliner, 2 Tea set, 3 Eligible, 4 Titbit, 5 Streets, 6 Deceased, 7 Surplus, 8 Notion, 9 Espouse, 10 Evolve.

## MISUNDERSTOOD

*Across*: 1 Literal, 7 Brain, 8 Averted, 9 Anchor, 11 Aspic, 13 Hang, 14 Ghastly, 15 Kegs, 16 Utter, 17 Staple, 21 Carrots, 22 Signs, 23 Details.
*Down*: 2 Investment, 3 Earnings, 4 Amen, 5 Grin, 6 Wish, 9 Abate, 10 Ornamental, 12 Badge, 13 Hysteria, 18 Avid, 19 Long, 20 Cake.

## DISEMBARKING

**Andrew Pennington**. Order leaving the steamer: First Simon Doyle, Second Jacqueline de Bellefort, Third Andrew Pennington, Fourth Salome Otterbourne, Fifth Tim Allerton.
Order returning to the steamer: First Andrew Pennington, Second Simon Doyle, Third Tim Allerton, Fourth Jacqueline de Bellefort, Fifth Salome Otterbourne.

# THE SUM OF A PYRAMID

7 is the only digit not to appear in row totals.

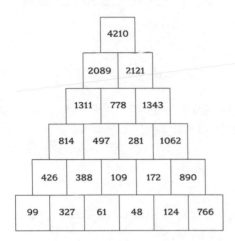

# VOWEL PLAY

Across:  7 Statue, 9 Oracle, 10 Coordinate, 11 Tide, 12 Eager,
13 Alignment, 15 Riveted, 20 Artichoke, 21 Heart, 23 Miss,
24 Transience, 25 Design, 26 Arrest.

Down: 1 Ottoman, 2 Stories, 3 Relic, 4 Foreigner, 5 Ragtime,
6 Eluding, 8 Pearl necklace, 14 Withstand, 16 Cruises, 17 Oilskin,
18 Meteors, 19 Precise, 22 Aswan.

## MASK-ERADE

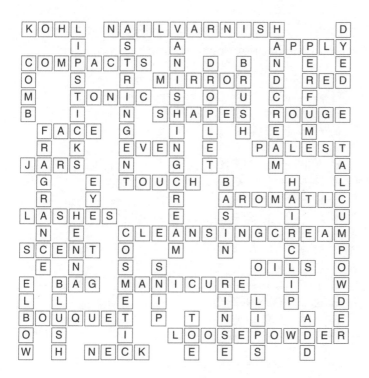

## BROUGHT TO BOOK

The book is on the fourth shelf down. It is the third book from the right.

## ANYONE FOR TENNIS?

At least six ladies would have all four items. Add the numbers of items on display together: 108 hats + 90 floral dresses + 112 necklaces + 56 parasols = 366. No lady can have two of any same item. The number of ladies times three items would equal three hundred and sixty items (120 x 3 = 360). There are six items still left (366 − 360 = 6). The least number of ladies to have all four items must be six.

## THE MAJESTIC HOTEL

The word **CASES** is hidden in the word search **THREE** times. The word **COURTYARD** is in the list but does not appear in the grid.

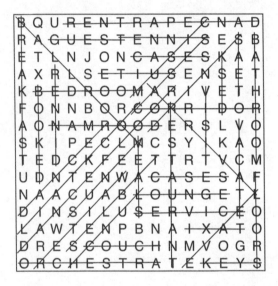

## RED HERRINGS

*Across:* 8 Cottage, 9 Floor, 10 Elder, 11 Diagram, 12 Book, 13 Children, 16 Suspects, 18 Hall, 21 Bluffed, 23 Topic, 25 Diner, 26 Unaware.
*Down:* 1 Acre, 2 Studio, 3 Marry, 4 Read, 5 Affable, 6 Horror, 7 Criminal, 12 Busybody, 14 Hat, 15 Perform, 17 Squint, 19 Appear, 20 Steal, 22 Drug, 24 Chef.

# CARDS ON THE TABLE

The final combination of cards totals 26.

A heart is worth six. A diamond is worth seven. A spade is worth eight. A club is worth nine.

The third row of cards shows a club and a diamond. They total 16. The value of each suit is different, so 8 + 8 is not a possibility. The two cards must be worth seven and nine. On the second row, if the club were worth seven, then both the hearts would have to be sevens as well (7 + 7 + 7 = 21) and that is not an option. The club must be worth nine, leaving the hearts to both be six (6 + 9 + 6 = 21). With the value of the club established as nine, the diamond on row two has to be worth seven (9 + 7 = 16). On the top row, the value of the diamond and the value of the heart are established. Take these away from the total to work out the value of the spade (21 − 7 − 6 = 8). This leaves the bottom row with a nine, an eight and a nine (9 + 8 + 9 = 26).

# TAKE YOUR PARTNERS

1 Tango, 2 Reel, 3 Conga, 4 Rumba, 5 Valse, 6 Veleta.

## ROUTE MAP

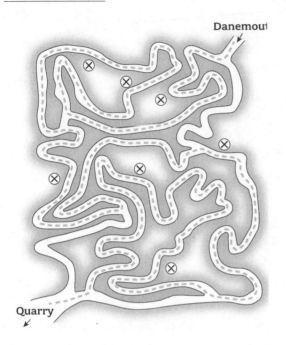

Danemout

Quarry

## LAST WILL AND TESTAMENT

Did you have the foresight? The writer of the will has hidden a message in every fourth word of this message.

I hope that **ALL** my friends, after **MY** death will acquire **FORTUNE**. Terms of my **WILL** mean everyone can **BENEFIT**. My very favourite **CHARITIES** deserve this. So, **CLOSE** as we are **TO** when you miss **ME**, I send you **BEST** and most heartfelt **WISHES**.

## MISS MARPLE'S WORDS

1 Sideboard, 2 Pseudonym, 3 Talkative, 4 Performer, 5 Hollywood, 6 Cameraman, 7 Thrilling, 8 Impatient, 9 Knowledge, 10 Fortnight, 11 Honeymoon.

The quotation by Miss Marple is: *'A well-bred girl would never turn up at a point-to-point in a silk flowered frock.'*

When the letters in the centre shaded column are rearranged, they spell out the name of Miss Marple's friend, Dolly Bantry.

## LETTER TRAIL

All groups are anagrams of THE BODY IN THE LIBRARY, except group 3, which has only one letter Y in it when it needs two.

# CHAPTER 9:
# MURDER ON THE ORIENT EXPRESS

## THE JOURNEY

**PARIS** is in the grid twice.

## ADDER

1 Bet + Ray = Betray, 2 Her + Ring = Herring,
3 Kid + Nap = Kidnap, 4 Just + Ice = Justice,
5 Scar + Let = Scarlet, 6 Head + Lines = Headlines,
7 But + Ton + Button, 8 Leg + End = Legend.

## SNOW STORM

| | | |
|---|---|---|
| ISLE | SNOW | MISS |
| SNOW | NAME | IRON |
| LOSE | OMEN | SOLO |
| EWER | WENT | SNOW |

## SHADOW QUOTE

1 Tobacco, 2 Holster, 3 Reverse, 4 Similar, 5 Mumbled, 6 Pistols,
7 Outside, 8 Stabbed, 9 Hostage, 10 Slipper.

Poirot says, *'The impossible cannot have happened therefore . . .
the impossible must be possible.'*

## TRAIN TRACKS

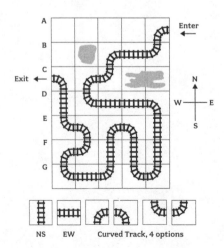

NS    EW    Curved Track, 4 options

# TRAVELLERS

Miss Worrall / Musician / Venice / 12 hours
Mr Delaney / Detective / Sofia / 8 hours
Mr Ryton / Teacher / Belgrade / 4 hours
Mrs Kravitz / Journalist / Milan / 20 hours
Mr Parker / Lawyer / Paris / 16 hours

# PIECE TOGETHER

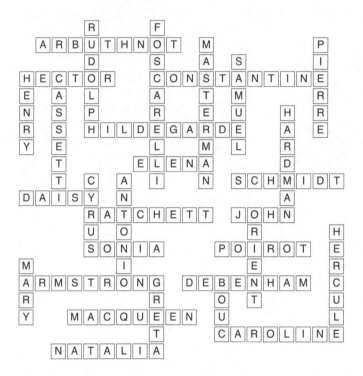

# SNOWFLAKES

*Top grid*: 1-2 Knife, 3-4 Often, 5-6 Berth, 7-8 Steam,
9-10 Wagon, 11-12 Count.
*Lower grid*: 1-2 Child, 3-4 Clock, 5-6 Occur, 7-8 Guard,
9-10 Train, 11-12 Night.

## ALIAS

*Across*: 7 Ransom, 8 Please, 10 Startle, 11 Eager, 12 Made, 13 Later, 17 Brain, 18 Once, 22 Wrong, 23 Escorts, 24 Reside, 25 Candle.
*Down*: 1 Presume, 2 Onwards, 3 Route, 4 Sleeper, 5 Range, 6 Hears, 9 Relatives, 14 Tragedy, 15 Intrude, 16 Feasted, 19 Swore, 20 Boast, 21 Ocean.

## DEADLY DOZEN

1 Eleven, 2 Two, 3 Ten, 4 Seven, 5 Four, 6 One, 7 Nine, 8 Five.

## ALL SHALL BE REVEALED...

The letters you seek: M, T, O, A, N, U, R, R, Y, A, U, Y /
YOUR AUNT MARY